Helping Them Heal

How Teachers Can Support
Young Children Who Experience
Stress and Trauma

Karen L. Peterson, PhD

Helping Them *Heal*

How Teachers Can
Support Young Children
Who Experience
Stress and Trauma

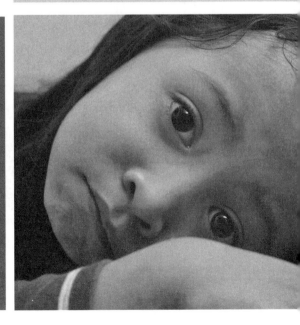

Karen L. Peterson, PhD

Gryphon House, Inc.
Lewisville, NC

Published by Gryphon House, Inc. P. O. Box 10, Lewisville, NC 27023. 800.638.0928; 877.638.7576 (fax). Visit us on the web at www.gryphonhouse.com.

Photographs courtesy of Shutterstock LP © 2012. All rights reserved. www.shutterstock.com.
Author photograph by Laura Evancich.

LIBRARY OF CONGRESS
CATALOGING-IN-PUBLICATION DATA

The Cataloging-in-Publication Data is registered with the Library of Congress for ISBN: 978-0-87659-475-9

BULK PURCHASE

Gryphon House books are available for special premiums and sales promotions as well as for fund-raising use. Special editions or book excerpts also can be created to specifications. For details, contact the Director of Marketing at Gryphon House.

DISCLAIMER

Gryphon House, Inc., cannot be held responsible for damage, mishap, or injury incurred during the use of or because of activities in this book. Appropriate and reasonable caution and adult supervision of children involved in activities and corresponding to the age and capability of each child involved are recommended at all times. Do not leave children unattended at any time. Observe safety and caution at all times.

Table of Contents

Acknowledgements

There are always many people who contribute to the writing and successful publication of a book, and that is most certainly the case with this one. I extend my appreciation and thanks to my editor, Stephanie Roselli, for her assistance, direction, and patience; to all of the editorial, design, and marketing staff at Gryphon House; and to Christi Hosking for her work on the annotated bibliography of children's books. I am grateful to the staff, children, and families of the Child Development Program at Washington State University, Vancouver, for allowing me the privilege of working with them "since the beginning." It is also important that I recognize the contributions of Dr. Chris Blodgett, Director, Washington State University Area Health Education Center (WSU Spokane), and his staff for their leadership and innovative work on behalf of trauma-affected children.

To the "Big 5" whom I consider my "invisible mentors"—Dr. Lilian Katz, Dr. Sherrill Richarz, Dr. Janice Fletcher, Dr. Pauline Zeece, and Karen Olson: My sincere thanks for sharing your vision and genuine respect for children and childhood. For their patience, understanding, and intellectual challenge, I express my appreciation to Laura Peterson and Dr. Jill Fancher. Most importantly, I express my deepest thanks to Jackie McReynolds, partner and colleague; for her help and encouragement I shall always be grateful.

Preface

Young children's need for engaging in creative, spontaneous play; having warm, caring interactions with interested and committed adults; and engaging in authentic activities, rich with experiences that pique intellectual curiosity, remains universal and unchanged. What has changed for a significant number of children, however, not only in the United States but across the globe, is the world in which children are growing up. These changes are marked by the exponential growth in information availability and use of technology, the continued rise in poverty with its limitations and barriers for families and communities, observable alterations to the natural environment, and a significant increase in the pace and complexity of life, even for young children. Accompanying these seemingly daunting realities are a multitude of positive changes and outcomes. What remains for many children is the issue of adapting to change while managing the intricate and complicated process of becoming a self-confident, self-reliant, and socially responsible individual. In short, growing up is more stressful than it once was.

For much of the past 25 years, stress and trauma has been a major focus of professionals in both the mental and physical health fields. Our awareness of the significance of its impact, as well as our general inability to successfully cope with stress, has been at the forefront of discussion and scientific investigation. Led by the innovative work that identified the adult-health outcomes from adverse childhood experiences, coupled with better diagnostic assessments of trauma effects, better understanding of chronic disease etiology, and greater agreement on the nature of developmentally appropriate practice, our appreciation of stress and its influence on children's development has become a topic of importance.

We know now that the number and kinds of experiences that are stressful and traumatic for young children are more widespread than previously known (or admitted) and that the detrimental effects of stress are more extensive and long lasting than we had

imagined. Contemporary research and practice have provided well-documented scientific and clinical evidence that support the need to strengthen prevention initiatives and intervention strategies focusing on children and their families. Translating this information (both research and practice) is an important task for those of us who work with children in preschool, child care, and kindergarten-elementary school settings where many (if not most) of the children affected by stress are located.

Over the past five years, I have given several trainings for early childhood professionals on understanding stress, complex trauma, and their effects on the development of young children. There continued to be strong interest, especially as presentations became more centered on classroom practice. I gave one of these presentations at a preconference session at the annual conference sponsored by the National Association for the Education of Young Children (NAEYC) in November 2011, where the focus was on supporting children in classroom settings—those places where stressed children find themselves being taught and cared for by adults who may be unaware of their experiences and the powerful effects of stress on development. This book was written as an expansion of that session and focuses on understanding stress and trauma, how professionals might approach their work with affected children, and suggestions for practice. While the contents highlight some of the ways early childhood professionals can help reduce the negative effects of stress and trauma, it is by no means a complete guide.

This book approaches the topic of working with children affected by stress and trauma with three goals in mind:
1. Provide readers with a research-based foundation on stress.
2. Offer suggestions for classroom practice that are based on real-life conditions.
3. Honor the work and commitment of early childhood professionals who give so much of their time, talent, and commitment to children.

Helping Them Heal

Chapters 1 and 2 provide background on stress, trauma, and their impact on children's development. Chapter 3 outlines ideas and approaches for focusing adult interactions and program planning that may best provide support for children's resiliency skills. Chapter 4 provides a series of ideas and questions focused on creating classroom community and how it can support children affected by stress. The content of Chapter 5 emphasizes the critical need to strengthen children's self-regulation skills as part of a comprehensive process for reducing stress impact. Chapter 6 is about building self-competence and self-efficacy as key ways to foster resiliency. Chapter 7 provides information on using literature as a tool for understanding, with an annotated book list presented in Appendix B. A reference bibliography and annotated resource list of books and articles and websites providing current and relevant information is provided at the end of the book.

This book is not intended to be used as a curriculum plan or therapy guide. It is my hope that the information and perspectives will provide answers, ideas, options for practice, and encouragement to those who work with young children. This book is dedicated to the proposition that all children are entitled to a childhood where curiosity, engagement, nurturance, and connection are at the forefront of experiences and where mature, thoughtful, caring adults who respect children and childhood can serve as their mentors, protectors, and partners. Most importantly, this book has been written for those teachers, assistants, adult students, directors, specialists, and other caring adults who work on behalf of preschool- and kindergarten-aged children each and every day.

Understanding Children's Stress and Trauma

FIVE THINGS WE KNOW

❶ Because a child's brain is growing and developing at such a rapid rate and is highly sensitive to overwhelming and disorganized sensory input, it is uniquely sensitive to the disruptive forces of stress and trauma.

❷ The child's brain develops quickly, with the newest areas supporting increased cognitive and behavioral function. Stress causes a decrease in the effectiveness of these "most used" and newest areas.

❸ Events that children experience do not have equal influence throughout development; there are periods where the brain is particularly sensitive to having too much or too little stimulation. This is especially true during the time when children are acquiring functional language skills.

❹ Stress hormones in the brain change how neural connections are made. Pruning or making connections between different areas of the brain determines our uniqueness. Stress hormones affect connections among emotional regulation, communication, and problem-solving areas.

❺ The child's brain is experience dependent—ordinary experiences of touch, sight, sound, and warm, engaging social connections with others are absolutely essential for building healthy connections among different parts of the brain.

Henry

Henry is four years old and has started his first month in Head Start. His biological father died during military service in Afghanistan when Henry was just two. His mother has recently remarried, and Henry now has an eight-year-old stepsister. His mother and new stepfather drink often on the weekends and argue loudly after Henry goes to bed. Sometimes no one is awake when he gets up in the morning. Henry has become more timid and also more angry and reactive with his stepfather and with other children in the apartment building where they live. His new stepsister is often angry and bullies him when no one is around. His grandfather (his biological father's father) visits and disapproves of his new stepfather and how Henry acts around him. Grandpa thinks Henry needs to "man up" and be more like his "real dad."

Many of us would consider Henry's situation to be stressful. Others may hold the opinion that arguing and fighting between parents is part of many children's lives. Children are considered hardy, resilient, and naturally equipped to adjust and move forward (Developing Child 2010; 2012a). The expectation is that events will be forgotten as the child enters school, makes new friends, and things settle down at home. While many people (usually those who are not familiar with the developmental needs of young children) do feel that stress in the lives of children is "just part of growing up," research and best practice provides a different picture (Chu and Lieberman, 2010).

What we do know is that stress is experienced in different ways for children of all ages, as compared with adults. Its impact is significant, long lasting, and important to address in the early years of growth and development. Stress and its partner, trauma, are part of many children's childhood experiences. Understanding what stress is, what are its sources, and how it is described is an important part of learning more about the lives of children who spend so much of their time in early childhood programs.

What Is Stress?

Stress is a part of every person's life. Its effect on children, their development, and their resulting behavior is one of the major challenges for most early childhood professionals. Stressed children react in a variety of ways that can make daily life in early childhood classrooms a bit chaotic, tense, and exhausting! Moreover, we all have somewhat different understandings of what stress is and what creates stressful situations for children.

The concept of *stress* was first introduced in the early 1900s in relation to understanding changes in metals: when an external force is applied (a strain), stress is the outcome. The term was later applied in connection to behavior and mental health (Selye, 1956). Stress refers to a response to stimulus. A *stressor* is any stimulation that causes a reaction or response that is above and beyond what the person is expecting or with which that person has had prior experience. Stress responses can be caused by loud noises, excessive hunger, fear of the dark, or being asked to speak in front of a group. Regardless of what the specific stressor may be, stressors always cause an imbalance in how the person is functioning (Rice, 1992). The person is then forced to adapt to the change in balance; it is this process of adapting that is stressful. While all living creatures experience the effects of stress as they grow and develop, our responses to stress are highly individualized. How a three-year-old responds will be different from the way a six-year-old may react when facing the exact same event or stressor. While there are typical responses to stress, such as jumping when the door suddenly slams, each individual responds in his own way. No two stress events are experienced in the same way.

Stress experiences can vary by a number of different criteria, based on how much impact stress experiences have had or may have on an individual. Stress experiences are often measured or described according to four criteria:

1. The amount of time that stress is experienced, from short-term (acute) to long-lasting (chronic)
2. The extent to which stress experiences are considered as part of everyday life, from ordinary and routine to those that are truly extreme
3. The level of impact or intensity, from positive (meeting a challenge that is within one's ability) to exceptionally negative (toxic)
4. The source of stress experiences, from internal (body pain, anxiety) to external (events happening directly and indirectly)

Developmental Stress

One way to better understand the effect of stress experiences on children is to consider the idea of developmental stress. Most early childhood professionals take a whole-child approach when looking at the developmental needs and abilities of young children (Hendrick, 2003). Additionally, we focus on attributes that children have within developmental domains: social, emotional, cognitive (including language), and physical (Bredekamp and Copple, 2009). The developmental "work" of a young child is twofold: to acquire skills and understandings in each of these domains and to coordinate these emerging abilities across domains.

Growth and change in each of these domains does not occur at the same rate. For example, it is typical for a four-year-old to have the physical skills of a five-year-old, the cognitive abilities of a four-year-old, but the social and emotional abilities of a three-and-a-half-year-old. Those newly acquired skills or understandings are most vulnerable to loss when a child is stressed or when a child is required to function at a high level. Developmental stress can occur when a child is expected to respond to demands that overtax at least two of these developmental domains at the same time; for example:

1. Asking a five-year-old to compete in a relay race (new experience for her) where she is given the rules verbally

(cognitive task requiring sequential thinking, language decoding, and memory for a novel task),

2. where she is then expected to speed walk to the other end of the play field (novel task requiring control and concentration along with a coordinated cognitive task requiring estimation of distance and placement of the body in space),

3. while trying to ignore or respond to friends shouting from the sidelines (dual requirements for emotional and social engagement and "screening out").

The combination of skills needed to complete the relay-race task requires that each domain operate at a maximum or top-level capacity at the same time. For this experience, the child is asked to utilize cognitive problem solving, language interpretation, physical control and coordination, and social engagement for a single coordinated and integrated event. Most likely, this event would not be a positive experience for a child who has any degree of self-doubt or inexperience. A negative outcome, such as not completing the race, forgetting the rules, being laughed at, or tripping, is an example of negative developmental stress. Negative reactions to developmental stress, which are usually very short term, decrease as children develop their skills and cognitive sophistication. Developmental stress is concerned with pushing those not-yet-coordinated domains beyond their capacity and explains why young children can be so easily thrown off-balance by seemingly "easy and fun" experiences.

Acute and Chronic Stress

Acute stress results from a single or limited experience; it is intense, sudden, and unexpected. Acute stress has an end, but it may vary in how long it takes to resolve. In most cases of acute stress, physiological balance is restored and children have the opportunity for recovery. For most children, their experiences with stress are usually acute. Responses to acute stress may occur immediately or may be somewhat delayed; for example, a child begins to get more clingy a day or two after a fire in her house. As the child develops an understanding of the event, she creates or uses familiar coping strategies to manage the disruption, fear, or unknown consequences of the event. Examples of acute stress include the following:

- undergoing medical tests or procedures,
- being chased or bitten by a dog,
- witnessing a car accident in which someone is hurt,
- nearly drowning,
- an encounter with a stranger who is drunk or mentally unstable, or
- getting lost for a period of time away from home.

Chronic stress includes experiences that are ongoing and pervasive. There is very little recovery time or opportunity to recover from repeated stress experiences. The types of events that occur in chronic stress are often unpredictable, multisensory, and occur within the child's immediate environment (Summers and Chazan-Cohen, 2012). Chronic stress experiences consist of multiple individual events, and it is the accumulation of these multiple experiences over time that results in a significantly different experience with stress.

The developmental characteristics of young children make them uniquely vulnerable to the persistent pressure, anxiety, and trauma that define chronic stress. Compared with those who undergo occasional acute stress, children who experience chronic stress face significantly greater negative outcomes. Of greater concern for many researchers and other clinical professionals is the understanding that much of the chronic stress children experience is at the toxic or traumatic level. Examples of chronic stress include the following:

- poverty and ongoing economic challenges,
- lack of essentials or other resources,
- community/neighborhood violence and the inability to escape or relocate,
- homelessness, even temporary,
- incarcerations or residential placement of parent or immediate family member,
- ongoing sexual, physical, or emotional abuse,
- chronic physical or emotional neglect,
- displacement, refugee status, or relocation,
- war and combat involvement or exposure,
- exposure to death, dying, and direct experience with grotesque images of events,
- witnessing violence in one's immediate environment, especially domestic violence,
- environmental devastation from floods, fire, earthquake, tornado damage, or toxic pollution.

Stress is a part of every person's life. Its effect on children, their development, and their resulting behavior is one of the major challenges for most early childhood professionals.

Positive and Negative Stress

Stress is also referred to in terms of the intensity or degree of impact. It begins with mild or positive stress and then builds to negative or toxic levels, peaking to the point of trauma.

FIGURE 1A

Stress Types and Responses			
Mild or Positive Stress	Tolerable or Moderate Stress	Toxic or Chronic Stress	Trauma
Push Forward	Concern, Anxiety	Hypervigilance, Fear	Terror, Flight-Fight-Freeze

(adapted from Perry, 1997; 2007)

While mild stress can be a motivator to push forward to meet deadlines, finish projects, or keep on schedule, more forceful stress can have more serious consequences. The effect of mild or positive stress is temporary, and its impact usually disappears once the deadline is met or a transition is made.

For children, positive stress may occur when they are asked to put on coats to go outside or put toys or projects away when they are not finished playing, when they have to delay play until Dad is finished grocery shopping, or they are told to take a bath when clearly (from the child's point of view) it is not needed. All of these mild or positive stressors provide a structure and build a series of behavioral expectations for children that are part of the socialization process. These mild stressors are intense only in the short run. They are manageable and generally predictable or familiar.

Most children have the skills and dispositions to manage these ongoing mild stressors without any negative consequences. While children may seem to overreact to these minor events, mild positive stress events do not result in behaviors that become a part of a negative or inappropriate pattern of coping. Parents and teachers play an important role in helping children recognize their successes in overcoming mild stress and learning to evaluate their efforts and accomplishments.

When stressors become more intense, based on the individual's awareness and perceived threat, the level of stress still remains manageable and is considered tolerable. In this state, the reaction results in feelings of anxiety, worry, and concern, which remain with the child for a longer period of time. Anxiety and worry occur when the child is aware and has had enough previous (negative) experience that she remains in a state of anxiety and concern. The uneasiness and apprehension continue until the child's level of physical and emotional distress is reduced or the threat ends. Young children usually focus their anxiety and worry on a potential loss or the expectation of a repeated negative experience. For example, Mom begins a new job, and the routines at home change; or Uncle Manuel was angry when he picked me up last night.

Will he be like that again today? These experiences are stress inducing because the child's reaction is focused on both stopping the physical feelings of loss or threat and worrying about the continuation of the experience in the future.

The next level of stress are those experiences so significant and pervasive (long lasting and/or intense) that they are toxic. Toxic stress experiences are so multisensory and intense that the child is unable to respond immediately or loses the ability to quickly regain a sense of balance and calm. The experiences of toxic stress create a physical and emotional reality of significant fear, ongoing threat, overwhelming physical and sensory stimulation, and instability.

What occurs for many children is a prolonged sensation of risk and fear that produces behaviors associated with hypervigilance. A hypervigilant child rarely relaxes and is on the lookout for more incidents of the initial stressor or stress event. This is especially true when the child experiences the same negative, intense event over time. In hypervigilance, the wariness and watchfulness take priority over playing with other children, eating with enjoyment, playing constructively, and ultimately trusting the intentions of other children and adults.

The last and most negative level of stress is that of trauma. Trauma stress is excessively intense, threatening, generally chaotic, overwhelming, and horrifying. As defined by Zero to Three (2012), *trauma* refers to "an event or events that involve actual or threatened death or serious injury to the child or others, or a threat to the psychological or physical integrity of the child or others." A child or adult who experiences a trauma event has little control over his physical and emotional responses to the event. The impact of this type of intense trauma is long lasting and can result in substantial physical and mental health issues for a developing child (Arnold and Fisch, 2011; Summers and Chazan-Cohen, 2012).

New research reveals that when toxic stress and trauma are experienced repeatedly, the impact on a child's development is significant and negative: the younger the child, the greater the negative impact (Arnold and Fisch, 2011). Events that are stressful for children, especially young children, are those which involve unexpected changes in their connections to other people and overwhelming negative sensory stimulation. Young children are not capable of "thinking through" stress and traumatic experiences; consequently, they receive a more intense effect than adults do.

Sources of Stress for Children

Any number of events, experiences, or actions of people can be stressful for children. Stressors can be physical, psychological (social-emotional-behavioral), and cognitive and are rarely "just physical" in nature. It is the association between the person and the experience that determines whether something is stressful. This is one reason why the same event to one person is experienced as "terrible" while the experience is thought to be "nonstressful" or "no big deal" by another.

What we do know is that stress-inducing experiences for children are different from those experienced by adults. These varying reactions are the result of the unique developmental characteristics that children possess. As children vary in age, temperament, experience, and cognitive style, they will differ in how they react to and respond to stress (Blaustein and Kinniburgh, 2010). Jason will experience the scary, barking dog next door differently at age three than he will at age six, simply because of his physiological maturity.

There are two major sources of stress for young children: internal and external (Jewett and Peterson, 2002). Within these two categories, any number of experiences can be stress inducing for children. Remember that some of the following experiences are considered acute while others are chronic. Children frequently experience combinations of acute and chronic stress simultaneously. For most children, the stressors are external but may result in symptoms and feelings of internal stress.

The stressors listed below are grouped by similarity of event to help provide some sense of organization and clarity. This list is certainly not a complete one but offers ideas for thinking about children's stressors.

Sensory Input

- pain
- bright light or darkness
- loud and/or unpredictable noise
- significant change in temperature
- unpleasant smell
- being pushed, shoved, hit, or threatened in a loud or violent way

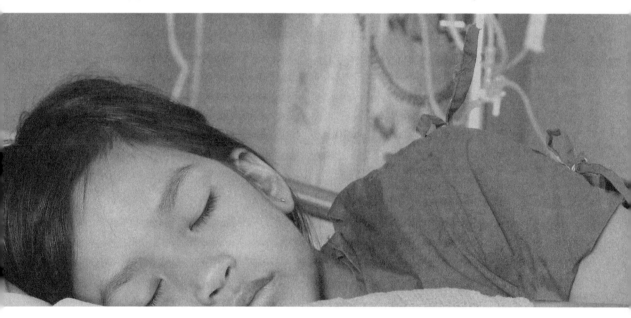

Self-Sufficiency Needs

- lack of control over food, water, clothing, and protection from weather
- unpleasant or toxic air quality
- unfit housing (place to sleep or play)
- having treatment for illness
- being confined in or abandoned in an unfamiliar place
- losing or having familiar objects taken away
- living in crowded conditions

Loss of or Change in Connection to Family and Familiar Friends

- incarceration
- death

- deployment
- separation or divorce
- parental mental health problems, such as depression, substance use or abuse
- abandonment
- remarriage
- new family members
- sibling loss (even temporary)
- death of a pet
- change in housing location
- going to a new school or child care program

Physical Injury*
- accidents
- acute or chronic illness
- abuse

* Includes injury experienced by other people in immediate contact with the child.

Social Issues within a Community
- poverty, violence, and disorganization
- lack of access to transportation
- isolation and overt discrimination by others
- witnessing violence and threats to others
- constant change in the neighborhood's physical makeup, such as construction, building/demolition, traffic, population shifts
- poor, inadequate, and/or unsafe housing, water, and/or sanitation
- lack of access to safe play spaces

All of these stressors share the combination of physical and emotional factors. As a result, children's reactions to stress will be seen in their emotional responses, social behaviors, ways of thinking, and in their physical sensations. Since all developmental domains are affected when stress is experienced, a child's response reflects this whole-body-and-mind impact.

Stress as a Multisensory Experience

Because both negative and positive experiences can lead to stress reactions, it is the intensity and duration of the feelings of imbalance that result in negative outcomes. Many events of living can be stressful for both adults and children, but children find events that are new and unique to be more troubling than a similar event may be for an adult (Loy, 2010). For example, a noninjury car accident is stressful for everyone involved, but the events for an adult will have a different stress impact. For an adult, stress can be cognitive as well as emotional: Does my insurance cover this? What will I do while the car is being repaired? Will this go on my driving record? Why did this happen to me? Wow, my neck hurts! Now, I am going to be late to work!

For a child, however, the experience will be focused on the overwhelming sensory stressors: the sound of the impact and the ensuing sirens, physical disorientation from the abrupt jolt of the accident itself, seeing and feeling the fear or anger expressed by the person driving. A child may feel trapped in the car seat; experience anxiety about being in an unfamiliar place with adults who are upset and angry; or endure a long wait sitting on the side of the road or waiting in a car while being hungry, without a favorite toy to ward off boredom, or needing to use the bathroom. Then, the child may be afraid that this whole experience will happen again.

The concept of stress was first introduced in the early 1900s in relation to understanding changes in metals: when an external force is applied (a strain), stress is the outcome.

For children, stress is never about a single stressor (hearing an unexpected loud noise, feeling the pain of being spanked, responding to someone else's anger and anxiety about being late to school); it is always a multisensory event. Stress for children happens to multiple areas of development at the same time and as a result has a more overwhelming impact (Stanford and Yamamoto, 2001). Experiences do not have to be direct, such as being slapped, but can be equally stressful and disturbing when defined as indirect, such as hearing parents fighting, witnessing an older child being hit or physically bullied, or being evicted from one's home (Summers and Chazan-Cohen, 2012).

For example, children who live in significant poverty are indirectly affected by the lack of resources for clothes, stable housing, and transportation. However, the stress experienced by the adults who care for them, the feelings of hunger, or constantly moving from place to place are direct stress and trauma experiences. Children are overwhelmed by these kinds of complex experiences because they lack social experience with the world, have limited cognitive abilities to apply complex thinking to cause and effect, and lack a fully integrated neurological system, making them highly sensitive to changes in their physical and sensory environments (Blaustein and Kinniburgh, 2010; Chu and Lieberman, 2010).

Vulnerability to Stress

All children experience stress and are at risk for its more negative effects. The impact of negative stress may be intensified, however, by two factors: the nature of the stress itself and the individual characteristics of the child. Any child's response to stress is unique and an expression of his age, genetic vulnerability, temperament, and in some situations, gender. Response levels of arousal, sensory intensity, the strength of his attachment system, prior experience with stress, and lack of opportunity to interact with an environment that is nonstressful play a role as well (Chu and Lieberman, 2010). Very young children, especially infants and toddlers, are most vulnerable due to their developmental immaturity. They are unable to regulate physical and emotional responses or to understand the causes and circumstances of their negative experiences. The coping patterns and responses that are adopted by very young children carry forward into behaviors in the preschool and early school years.

TEMPERAMENT

Temperament refers to the ways a person responds and adapts to the events of daily life. A person's temperament is biologically based, appears in infancy, and is relatively stable throughout life. It is determined by how a person responds according to certain characteristics:

- degree of sensitivity to sensory stimulation
- intensity of response to stimulation and circumstance
- activity and movement level
- approach to or withdrawal from new situations
- persistence in continuing with activities
- predictability of patterns of sleep, activity, bodily functions (also called *rhythmicity*)
- overall quality of mood
- distractibility

Janice Katz identifies three types of temperament: easy, cautious, and difficult. A person's temperament is remarkably consistent across settings, so a child who is easygoing at home will generally be easygoing at school. Temperament plays a major role in children's capacity to adapt, make friends, and manage the effects of stress.

Measuring Stress

There are no specific medical tests to determine whether a child has experienced a certain type of stress. Experts do know that experiencing stress elevates the heart rate; increases shallow breathing; causes restricted blood flow to the arms and legs; increases blood flow in the trunk of the body; increases the presence of stress-related hormones; and reduces the activity in multiple sections of the brain that manage areas of problem solving, memory, sensory integration, and emotional regulation.

At risk: having a greater potential of vulnerability to conditions and experiences that endanger or compromise health and development

Stress and trauma place children at risk for possible negative outcomes for all domains of development—social, physical, emotional, and cognitive. However, being at risk does not mean negative outcomes are certain, just more likely to occur (Osofsky, 2004).

Understanding the extent of a child's stress experiences (acute and tolerable versus chronic and toxic) is important when professionals are trying to determine the extent of a person's stress experiences or history. For adults, the Holmes and Rahe (1967) Social Readjustment Scale is frequently used (see Appendix A for an adapted copy). The scale lists multiple occurrences of life experience (for example, death of a spouse, loss of employment), and then assigns each a ranking of stress impact. The greater the total number of life-stress events, the greater that person's experience with stress is likely to be. More importantly, the greater the experience of stress, the greater its impact on the individual's physical and mental health and general well-being (Karr-Morse, 2012).

For children, one measure of stress experiences used by mental health professionals is the Trauma Symptoms Checklist for Young Children (Briere, 2005). It lists a number of life-stress experiences that are specific to childhood. This scale is used with elementary-aged children but is not generally used with preschool children. Self-report of experiences by parents and other significant adults is the method used in most settings for determining the extent of stress experiences and assumed impact for children. It is well known that traumatic and stress events that affect parents also affect their children (Chu and Lieberman, 2010). For early childhood professionals, it may be important to look beyond the experiences of the child and consider the experiences of the family as a primary source of information.

Helping Them Heal

Complex Trauma:

A Special Type of Stress

Complex trauma is the term for multiple stress-related life events experienced by a child. While similar to toxic or chronic stress, complex trauma describes a broader kind of negative experience that comes with multiple, repetitive events that occur within the intimate, caregiving circle between birth and five years of age. The effects are long lasting (O'Neill et al., 2010).

For example, we know that living in poverty results in multiple kinds of stress for many people, especially children. While stress is used to describe more specific responses to events, complex trauma focuses on understanding the integrated experiences of multiple kinds of negative events. Someone who has experienced complex trauma may have many experiences with violence, may have suffered corporal punishment as a child, may have lost a parent to death or incarceration, or may have endured prolonged poverty. The effect of these toxic experiences is cumulative. Medical researchers Robert Anda and Vincent Felitti developed the Adverse Childhood Experiences (ACE) Scale as part of a groundbreaking research study looking at health outcomes for adults. Items on the scale include such events as physical neglect, incarceration of a parent, and parental divorce. Studies indicate that adults who experienced at least four of these events show significant negative outcomes in mental and physical health in adulthood. It is not necessarily the intensity, duration, or potential physical negativity of these events, but the variety and total number in childhood that is associated with potential negative outcomes for adults (Arnold and Fisch, 2011; Blaustein and Kinniburgh, 2010). Multiple incidents with adverse childhood experiences have significant long-term health effects on individual well-being, capacity to manage relationships, significant risk-taking behavior, engaging in healthy life choices, and securing and sustaining productive employment (www.acestudy.org).

A stressor is any stimulation that causes a reaction or response that is above and beyond what the person is expecting or with which that person has had prior experience.

Why Is It Important to Address the Impact of Stress on Young Children?

We know most children can adapt and recover from moderate levels of stress and show no known negative long-term outcomes. But, we also know that young children who experience persistent, especially toxic, or enduring tolerable stress will display behaviors that are often not constructive and are damaging to themselves and their relationships with others. Not only does stress force children to adapt in ways that may not be in their best interest, but stress effects also pose problems for their physical health. Children acquire and build responses to stress that become long-term coping strategies. These strategies will remain part of the child's behavioral repertoire because children have little control over how they respond and what they understand. These coping behaviors are resistant to change, and children often use them in situations where such strong reactions are not appropriate or even effective.

Persistent and toxic stress also impairs a child's ability to problem solve or to "read" the environment accurately and to move comfortably from one setting or event to another. These characteristics are long lasting and affect children's potential for leading productive social lives, learning in school settings, and understanding and managing their own feelings. With greater understanding of the mechanics of how stress and trauma work and how children cope with stress and trauma, we are closer to developing intervention strategies and techniques that may be helpful to children.

Ideas for Practice

Consider each of the following situations, which are taken from real-life experiences. For each example, identify the category of stress experienced by the child: mild, tolerable, toxic, trauma, and complex trauma. Then, identify the developmental domain(s) that are impacted: cognitive, physical, social, and/or emotional.

Helping Them Heal

1. Nancy, five years old, was bitten on the hands and face by a neighborhood dog that ran into her front yard where she was playing with her nine-year-old brother.

2. Sanji, three years old, had tubes placed in his ears to stop his frequent ear infections.

3. Gerald, six years old, was moved to his third foster home last week. He was placed in foster care after his father's girlfriend was arrested for physically abusing him and his younger sister over a period of two years.

4. Nathan, five years old, was on the way to kindergarten when the family car stalled on the road; Grandma came and picked him up and took him to school.

5. Remy, four years old, has just moved to a new apartment in the neighborhood where his family has always lived. This new place is smaller and has no heat, and Remy shares a room with two siblings. He says the neighborhood is scary and loud, and he worries about his dad riding the bus to work.

6. Kate, five years old, is in kindergarten. After six hours of school time, she has lessons each week (depending on the season) for gymnastics, soccer, or T-ball. She always goes to piano on Tuesdays and stays with a sitter on Wednesday and Friday until 7 p.m., when her grandma picks her up for alternate weekend visits with her separated parents.

7. Mason, four years old, often wets the bed. His parents are taking him to the urologist at the hospital who will examine him. After the exam, he will have an MRI and lab work.

8. Mari, four years old, is a newly immigrated child from Indonesia. She was three when earthquakes leveled her house and killed her grandfather. She speaks little English and has never been in a preschool before.

9. Marcelo, six years old, is in kindergarten and spends each summer with extended family outside of the United States. The community where his extended family lives is overrun with violent gang activity. There have been kidnappings, shootings, and people hurt going to the park and grocery store.

For children, stress is never about a single stressor (hearing an unexpected loud noise, feeling the pain of being spanked, responding to someone else's anger and anxiety about being late to school); it is always a multisensory event.

10. Simon, three years old, is just about to turn four. He was watching out the window of his apartment when he saw and heard the lady across the street hit and killed by a car. Her body was in the street for a long time; the police and medical people were there and lots of other people were talking, crying, and yelling.

Situation	Stressor Event	Level of Stress or Trauma	Domain(s) Impacted
1. Nancy			
2. Sanji			
3. Gerald			
4. Nathan			
5. Remy			
6. Kate			
7. Mason			
8. Mari			
9. Marcelo			
10. Simon			

The Mechanics of
Stress and
Trauma

FIVE THINGS WE KNOW

❶ Stress is a physiological event for children over which they have little or no control and few skills to manage.

❷ The impact of stress on children varies by intensity and ranges from mild to moderate to toxic.

❸ Most negative effects of stress come from repeated experiences.

❹ Children's experiences with stress result in heightened sensory sensitivity, disorganization, and persistent fear and anxiety.

❺ Experiences with stress result in reduced capacity and skill to think through experiences and find solutions to problems, reduced levels of self-awareness and self-efficacy, and poorer social and emotional regulation skills.

How Do Children
Experience Stress and Trauma?

Over the past decade, our understanding of the physical impact of stress and trauma on children's development has increased substantially. Advances in brain and body imaging, as well as better measures that assess behavior, have provided clearer information on how stress and trauma work. For children, stress and trauma are always physical experiences, even though they most often seem to be about feelings. It is this physical impact that takes its toll on young children, disrupting physical, emotional, and cognitive development (Developing Child 2004a; 2010).

Whether a child experiences being yelled at by an adult, a car accident without injury, living with a lack of food or a place to sleep, or not knowing where his family is, these events have the same process in common. Experiences of stress and trauma originate in our physical reaction to sensory input or stimulus from the outside (Chu and Lieberman, 2010; Developing Child 2009; 2010). Stress and trauma always involve a short- or long-term disruption to the balance of a child's life through the body's experience of negative events.

When a child experiences sensations—both negative and positive—the central nervous system and brain are the primary players. The central nervous system, made up of the brain and spinal cord, responds to information that is perceived through the senses. For example, when a child witnesses someone close by being yelled at and slapped, the experience is felt first as a physical event and second as an emotional event. The child's senses receive the intensity and volume in sound (yelling and the smack of hitting) coupled with the feeling of physical threat (crowding and pushing), and finally the emotional impact of threat and fear. Physical and emotional sensations come with the experience of stress—butterflies in the stomach; increased heart rate; and feeling upset, agitated, or frightened. These are the body's way of protecting and preparing us for a very basic, nonnegotiable fight,

Helping Them Heal

flight, or freeze response.

Responses to sensory stimulation are stronger and more intense for young children than for adults. While it may appear that children are oblivious to what is going on around them, their senses remain highly attuned to changes in smell, taste, touch, sight, and sound. For children, integrating sensory information causes part of their distress. In a stress or trauma experience, the visual images may not be linked in the brain with the sounds and physical sensations of the event. What may result is a more intense and overwhelming experience.

Experience Filters

Children are, first and foremost, sensory and physical beings. They process and understand their world through three experience filters:

- sensory-physical
- social-emotional
- thinking and understanding

For children, stress and trauma are always physical experiences, even though they most often seem to be about feelings.

Filters of experience modify how and what a child comprehends and influence feelings, interactions, events, and, ultimately, herself as a person. Each filter receives information that passed through the prior filter; as a result, each is then vulnerable to "scratching or warping." The condition of the sensory-physical filter affects the image and information that is passed onto the social-emotional filter, and then along to the thinking-cognitive filter. Experiences of stress and trauma alter the condition of each of these filters, and the first two filters are the most affected.

As children develop greater cognitive capacity, the thinking filter becomes more influential while remaining strongly affected by both the sensory-physical and social-emotional filters. Awareness of these filters can help adults understand why the cumulative experiences of stress and trauma cause so much damage. Adults who want to assist stress- and trauma-affected children must pay attention to the altered images and experiences that have been changed through experiences at each of these filter levels. Trying to intervene at the thinking and understanding filter level may not be successful if the distortions that have been absorbed by the first two filters are not addressed. For example, supporting the sensory-physical filter so that it provides consistent, reasonably accurate, and balanced images of what children experience is to evaluate how children experience the environment through vision, hearing, touch, and smell. Helping children learn to calm themselves when they are anxious and expanding their familiarity (as well as their sensory vocabulary) with different types of sensory experiences can provide ways to strengthen their positive interactions and offset those experiences that trigger more familiar negative ones.

For example, when children are in a small group setting, teachers can talk them through observations of their sensory surroundings.

By drawing attention to visual, auditory, tactile, and even olfactory sensations and by using descriptive vocabulary, teachers can increase children's awareness and cognitive capacity. Learning to isolate sensations creates awareness and builds thinking skills. Children's experience filters are often clouded with a mix of sensory input, emotional responses, and cognitive confusion; developing more objective awareness can bring greater clarity and understanding over time. A discussion could begin with a teacher's comments, such as the following:

- "I see the sunlight coming in the window today. I think (or feel) that it brings more light and warmth into the classroom."
- "I am going to close my eyes for a minute and just listen to what I can hear in the classroom. I can hear children's voices

talking. Some voices are quiet and some sound excited. These sounds tell me there is lots of play and 'getting along' among the other children. What else do you hear when you close your eyes? What do those sounds tell you?"

- "For just a minute I am going to pay close attention to my feet! If I close my eyes and think about my feet, what do you think I might feel? Think about your feet. Are your toes touching each other inside your shoes? Are your feet feeling warm? How do your feet know that you have on shoes?"

FILTERS

Filters change how we perceive and subsequently understand what we are seeing or hearing. When used with technology such as cameras, filters protect, enhance, alter, and sometimes erase visual or auditory sensations. Sometimes just a single filter is used, but more often multiple filters create a view of the world that appears more complex and sensational.

Filters are vulnerable, however, if scratched or warped; they cause distortion, resulting in images that are blurred, out of proportion, and more intense than the eye (and brain) can comprehend. While we know filters enhance both negative and positive images, we must be aware of their potential for vulnerability.

Filters of experience also provide a protective "shield" for helping us cope with many potentially overwhelming events. For example, our ability to think through a stressful event (activating the thinking filter) can buffer sensations absorbed by the sensory-physical filter. When we possess thinking strategies that help us strategically get out of a stressful situation, our thinking filter is in focus and can override the powerful input from sensory-physical information.

All stress begins in the body— the receiving center for all sensory stimuli. As sensory data are processed by the nerves in our skin, ears, eyes, mouth, and nose, this information is transmitted through the central nervous system to various parts of the brain. Young children, whose nervous systems are not fully developed and integrated, feel sensory information intensely and immediately. Not only does this result in sensory patterns that deliver strong impulses to the brain, but it also means that the body itself responds intensely. Stress impact on children is felt first as a physical response; then, emotions come as a reaction to these physical sensations (Grasso et al., 2012; Gunnar et al., 2009).

The brain receives signals of threat, tension, and sensory intensity. In response, the nervous system sends out impulses to the smooth muscles and glands. The body releases stress hormones: adrenaline, cortisol, and related hormones. The presence of adrenaline and cortisol in the bloodstream results in increased heart rate and breathing, constriction in the veins of the skin (feeling the chills), tense muscles, restriction of blood flow to the outer areas of the body (hands and feet get colder), slowed digestion, and decreased general problem-solving capabilities (Loy, 2010; Rice, 1992).

This primes the body for protection and keeping itself away from both real and perceived threat. Not only do these stress hormones cause changes to occur within the body itself, but they also cause changes within the brain. The body's response to the influx of hormones and muscle changes is to ready itself to defeat the perceived threat or react to the intense sensory input. The human body remains in this active state—known as the

FIGHT, FLIGHT, OR FREEZE

FIGHT: Physiological arousal and aggression—irritability, anger, trouble concentrating, hyperactivity, or silliness

FLIGHT: Withdrawal and escape—social avoidance and isolation, sitting alone in class or outdoors

FREEZE: Stilling and constriction—restrained emotional expression, quiet or static behavior, overcompliance, and denial of needs

Source: Blaustein and Kinniburgh (2010)

fight, flight, or freeze response—until the danger is over. In cases of acute or short-term stress, the hormones are reabsorbed and released from the body and balance is restored (Katz, 2013).

The process of establishing hormonal and physical balance occurs over time; it is not an immediate process. Children who have several stress experiences may need several hours or days for their bodies to restore themselves to a more typical pattern of functioning. A child who has a highly stressed morning before coming to school will come to school stressed and remain so for several hours. His behavior, even in nonstressed settings, will reflect the prior events and their lingering effects. Figure 2A illustrates the impact of the varying levels of stress on the body and brain.

We know most children can adapt and recover from moderate levels of stress and show no known negative long-term outcomes.

Stress and Perceived Threat Level	Low, Positive	Moderate, Tolerable	Toxic/Chronic	High, Trauma
Adaptive response	Receptive, ready to learn and adjust	Aware, cautious, concerned	Freeze, withdrawal, or flight-fight	Terror, flight-fight-freeze
(Brain) Thinking capacity	Abstract, creative, planned ideas and strategies	Concrete ideas; use of known ideas and strategies	Emotionally focused strategies	Reactive-reflexive responses; self-defense strategies
Physical state	Calm, interested, engaged	Arousal attention, anxious	Alarm, fear, hypervigilance	Panic, terror

(adapted from Perry, 1997; 2007)

The Body-Brain Connection and Stress

The brain functions as an interconnected system, carrying information through electrochemical signals across different areas. When not in a stressed condition, these essential connections support creative problem solving, formation of positive social interactions, learning of new skills and language, and display of coordinated physical skills (Developing Child 2009, 2010). An unstressed brain is the essence of a child who is curious, engaged with others, physically active, and usually emotionally stable.

When stress is introduced, connections between the different areas of the brain may be overconnected (too much stimulation), underconnected (lacking in stimulation), or misdirected. This stress-induced brain activity results in feelings, behavior, and thinking that reflect the disruption and chaos that is occurring as the body attempts to rebalance itself. What makes a person feel "stressed-out" is not just the electrochemical reaction of the nervous system and brain to an upsetting event: it is also the changes in how the brain functions when it responds. During a threatening event, the brain activates stress hormones as a way to attempt to regain balance, and this response process is repeated each time stress is perceived, whether real or imagined. Sensitivity to stress is often activated by a sensory trigger. Triggers for stress can be immediately present (right in front of the child) or the result of a sensory awareness of stimuli (smell, sound, visual image) associated with a previous experience (Katz, 2013). For example, if a child experiences being physically threatened and pushed, then later she may have feelings of panic in a crowded play space where no real threat is present. Triggers—any stimuli that serve as a sensory reminder of past experiences—for stress responses remain for long periods of time and are often difficult to both identify and reduce or stop. They may be external (being yelled at, smells, or locations) or internal (feeling hungry or feeling anxious in front of a group) or may be combinations of internal and external (Blaustein and Kinniburgh, 2010; Katz, 2013).

While the brain plays a critical role in the body's perception of and response to stress, scientists are not certain how different areas of the developing child's brain responds to varying types of stimulation. However, they do know that areas of the brain that regulate input, problem solving, intensity of physical reactions, communication, and memory are all negatively affected by stress and trauma (Arnold and Fisch, 2011; Developing Child 2008, 2009; Katz, 2013).

Stress affects the brain's ability to pass sensory messages between its left and right hemispheres. This is one of the primary reasons for the decrease in a child's ability to problem solve, use language to moderate behavior, and regulate his emotions. The structure

Helping Them Heal

that joins the two halves of the brain, the corpus callosum, becomes less capable of helping sensory messages travel between the different regions when the person is experiencing stress. Brain imaging has shown that when children experience significant stress, the corpus callosum is actually smaller in size (Developing Child, 2009). Stress diminishes the capacity of the executive function of the brain to make decisions, prioritize, plan, organize, communicate effectively with others, shift between tasks, hold and use new information, and adapt to situations in which behavior must be modified (Developing Child, 2009, 2011; Karr-Morse, 2012).

Prolonged activation of the body's stress-response system has significant negative effects.

Long-Term Exposure to Stress and Trauma

Prolonged activation of the body's stress-response system has significant negative effects. In the case of toxic and chronic stress and trauma, the stress-response system remains hyperalert after significant events are over. For example, a child's repeated exposure to domestic violence results in lasting increased levels of cortisol and stress responses (Biglan et al., 2012; Grasso et al., 2012). Reoccurring experiences of stress are not just added onto the body and brain's initial response but are experienced as new stress responses. In other words, the entire sequence of arousal, hormonal release, and body and brain response are repeated each time the child experiences threat and intensity. The repeated activation of stress and intense sensory stimulation results in hypersensitivity and exhaustion. The body simply is unable to maintain its heightened activation and is overtaxed and unable to return for a period of time to a balanced state. Having the body continuously or chronically in a state of stress arousal has significant negative outcomes for the individual and the body itself (Arnold and Fisch, 2011; Biglan et al., 2012; Developing Child, 2009; Osofsky, 2004).

Long-term experiences of chronic and toxic stress adversely affect the immune system and the functional capacity of the brain (Developing Child 2009; 2010). Evidence indicates that high levels of stress in very young children (infants in particular) can lead to change in how the brain functions and in the architecture of the brain itself (Arnold and Fisch, 2011; Developing Child 2009; Osofsky, 2004). Studies have shown that toxic levels of stress alter areas of the brain that regulate certain executive skills. Some areas, particularly those that normalize emotional regulation, have been found to be smaller in size, while areas that manage threat responses have been found to be disproportionally larger.

Childhood experiences of chronic, toxic stress and trauma affect later adult physical and mental health—for example, chronic fatigue, headaches, irritable bowel syndrome, ulcers, suppressed immune system, increased risk of heart attack and stroke, increase in alcohol and substance abuse, smoking, obesity, and significant increased vulnerability to anxiety and depression disorders (Arnold and Fisch, 2011; Blaustein and Kinniburgh, 2010). Consequently, learning to manage the physical and emotional responses to stress in childhood is important. A long-term approach to reducing the impact of negative stress involves decreasing exposure in the first place as well as reducing the physiological impact (Blair and Raver, 2012; Developing Child, 2011).

How Do Children Respond to Stress?

Children's reactions to stress occur through a series of stages. Each stage builds on the previous one and places different demands on the child (Marion, 2011).

Stage One: Alarm

The beginning phase of stress response occurs when the child becomes aware of a threat. Alarm means the child is absorbing the emotional and physical information from the potential stressor. Alarm is not rational and may be the result of a physical response to a previous stress trigger or cue.

Jamie

Jamie hears the door slam about the time when his big brother comes home from work. In the past, his brother has yelled at him and has kicked his toys across the room after coming home. The alarm occurs when Jamie hears the door slam, even though the door slam might not be the result of his brother's actions. Door slams and loud noises are probably always stressors for Jamie.

Stage Two: Appraisal

In this stage, the child assesses the stressor and the event in relationship to what her past experience has been. Marion (2011) notes that the child's appraisal is affected by developmental characteristics for memory and understanding; previous experience with the stressor; and the prior responses that significant adults have displayed in reaction to the same or similar stressors—for example, anger, fear, or neutral feedback. Stress appraisal also involves the child's self-efficacy (the feeling and understanding that she can be effective in the choices she makes and the actions she takes) and self-awareness (the extent to which the child assumes that she is part of the event).

The role of rational thinking skills is limited by the impact of stress hormones and processing changes that occur in the brain at most phases of the stress-response cycle. Reactions and responses at this stage are physiological, sensory, and emotional and reflect a system that is trying to rebalance with little input from the thoughtful part of the brain. For children, their responses are even more fear, threat, flight, freeze, panic, worry, and terror.

José

Children in stage two may display behavior where they respond in fearful ways to events that seem unrelated to their stressor. For example, after being in a minor car accident with his grandmother, José seems afraid of all large moving vehicles. He is cautious and anxious when in the car, and he screams when he sees a fast-moving truck. José's reaction is a response to his stress-coping patterns that became overly reactive or sensitive to the physical-sensory stimulation that overwhelmed him at the time of the accident.

Stage Three: Coping

The final stage of stress response is that of creating or searching for ways to deal with the recognized stressor. Children, like adults, use coping mechanisms to reestablish the feeling of balance. The goal is to reduce the feelings that occurred in the previous stage and to prevent any further occurrence. Coping strategies are simply responses that may have little to do with their effectiveness in preventing another incident. For some children, their "balanced state" is one of agitation or worry. Being angry, withdrawn, belligerent, or anxious is more familiar (and thus calming) than behaviors that are assumed to be more stable and socially acceptable. Stressed and traumatized children cope with real and perceived threat by acting in a variety of ways they believe will keep them safe. Coping strategies used by young children are based on very simple, basic physical and emotional feelings and reactions (Katz, 2013; Steele and Malchiodi, 2012).

Maria

At lunch Maria, who is four, hits Juan hard enough that he falls off his chair. She says that he sat too close to her and it seemed like he wanted to take her crackers. Taken at face value, her intense response may look like an overreaction. Yet, Maria's response may be the result of previous experiences and use of a behavior that (from her perspective) works. At home, Maria has been pushed and teased by her grandfather about her eating habits. Her behavior (hitting back) does make her grandfather move away; although, he continues to tease her and use his loud voice. In her response to Juan, Maria has experienced alarm and appraisal and has responded with a coping strategy.

The three stages of stress response occur in order but may vary in how rapidly they are covered. A child may make several attempts at using different coping strategies in stage three. It may take time for him to find or invent a strategy that feels effective in restoring the sense of balance. The child's use of coping or response strategies has little to do with their realistic effectiveness but everything to do with prior use, lack of skill, perceived success, and physical discomfort. As important as it is for early childhood professionals to recognize these stages of adaptation, it is essential for them to know what kinds of stressors and events negatively affect young children.

ARE SOME CHILDREN JUST MORE STRESSED?

Children who are sensitive to their physical environment and are emotionally reactive may be more vulnerable to the effects of stress. The anxious child may have a strong sense of responsibility, high standards of achievement, difficulty relaxing, tendency to please others, difficulty with assertiveness, oversensitivity to criticism, and a tendency to worry (Foxman, 2004). While sometimes more challenging to deal with, anxious children are usually successful and interested in learning and school; are generally kind, loyal, and caring with friends; and may display any number of hidden interests and talents. The anxious child is one who seeks to know the outcome of events well in advance. Reassurance and preparation are key teaching strategies for strengthening confidence and lessening worry in these children.

Symptoms or signs of stress and trauma may be behavioral, emotional, cognitive, or physical. For preschool and young school-age children, coping strategies typically are a combination of physical, emotional, and cognitive responses. Children's reactions to emotional and physical stress are an attempt to rebalance, to get back to or to seek some sense of steadiness. Seeking to secure this sense of balance is physically exhausting, emotionally draining, and often fear inducing (Stanford and Yamamoto, 2001).

CHILDREN'S RESPONSES TO STRESS

- Passive: excessive fatigue, withdrawing from activities (pulling away, wandering), displaying fear or hesitancy
- Self-focused behaviors: nail biting, wringing hands, twisting hair, biting lips, repetitive whole-body movements (especially feet)
- Interactions with others: stuttering, bullying, threatening, hurting others, laughing nervously or inappropriately, pestering others
- Interactions with objects: excessive squeezing or tapping of pencils, clumsy or fumbling actions with hands and fingers

Source: Marion (2011)

The "stress of stress" shows in children's physical reactions. Children who are stressed, either at the positive (tolerable) or negative levels, may do any of the following:

- have problems with sleeping, such as waking in the middle of the night, difficulty falling asleep or waking up, and having fears about sleeping;

- have difficulties with eating, such as not wanting to try new foods, being overly picky, being anxious about having enough to eat, or hoarding food and treats;
- withdraw from play and interactions with others and prefer to be alone in most situations;
- resist following simple rules (especially those that are routine) and protest changes in routines (even those that are familiar);
- avoid taking care of personal needs, such as resistance to putting on clothes, using the toilet properly, or putting toys and things away;
- be overly controlling about toys and possessions, hiding or hoarding them;
- display nervous habits, such as sucking on fingers or rocking or constantly moving around, especially with facial expressions that are tense and strained;
- be overly aggressive, especially when seemingly unprovoked;
- interrupt and cause disorder to other children's activities and games, destroy or tear apart work in progress such as projects and block structures;
- show an inability to relax or agitation and anxiety in situations that are familiar and routine;
- appear to be constantly overwhelmed, crying for "no reason," or worrying most of the time;
- exhibit signs of separation, sadness, loss and grief, or be withdrawn, cheerless, and distressed for more than a few days;
- display hypervigilance, watching what others are doing much of the time, asking about other children or adults, or frequently asking, "What happened to_____?" "What's next?" and "Where did you go?"
- show indications of cognitive disorganization, such as an inability to focus or concentrate on familiar and well-liked activities, poor short-term recall or memory, confusion in problem-solving, or impulsivity in decision making;
- complain of physical discomfort (stomachache, headache, fatigue, pain) when there does not seem to be a physical reason.

Sources: Arnold and Fisch, 2011; Loy, 2010; Osofsky, 2004; Summers and Chazan-Cohen; 2012

What Do Children Learn from Stress?

Children learn with every new experience and interaction. Positive or low-to-moderate stress has the potential for positive outcomes for children, such as meeting appropriate challenges, mastery of manageable conflicts, and tests of personal strength and persistence. Stress in its positive or even moderate forms results in the development of essential coping skills, intellectual skills, and understandings that most children acquire.

The negative outcomes of stress center on children's sensitivity to the behavior and perceived intention of others. Unlike adults, children do not have cognitive or physical capacities to regulate their physiological responses, reduce threat, or remove themselves from threat (Developing Child, 2011). When stress is chronic, toxic, or traumatic, children learn through their own limited understanding of the circumstances and their physical-emotional responses (as well as those of the adults around them) to respond in the following ways:

- **Be wary of others.** This results in interference with healthy, secure attachments and trust; hurtful experiences become the stuff of emotional memories, and rejection becomes expected.
- **Act in self-defense first.** This limits the development of social skills and helpful, constructive interactions with other children and adults; friends are few and far between, and adults are to be approached with caution.
- **Be afraid almost all the time.** This leads to an inability to differentiate between threat and safety, thus limiting children's experiences of curiosity, enjoyment, and peace. Hypervigilance is tiring and confining.
- **Think with a cluttered mind.** This leads to difficulty focusing on tasks at hand and making thoughtful decisions about what's next. This limits the use of language that helps expand understanding, inhibits remembering details and seeing how parts fit together, and restricts what can be learned during the most critical years of intellectual development.

FEAR

One of the primary feelings children learn from stress and, especially, trauma is fear—worry, anxiety, and dread. Mental health professionals now know that children do not naturally outgrow early learned fear responses (Developing Child, 2010). More importantly, simple removal of a child from a stressful environment does not necessarily reverse negative impacts of early learning and early fear responses. A child must adopt new methods of coping and have repeated experiences with more positive feelings to overcome the permanence of fear.

A New Model for Working with Stressed and Traumatized Children

Trauma-informed care offers a way to provide support, increase essential coping skills, and strengthen resilience in children who are experiencing or have experienced stress and trauma (Steele and Malchiodi, 2012; Blaustein and Kinniburgh, 2010). This approach is especially focused on the impact of chronic, toxic stress and trauma.

Trauma-informed practice provides a series of principles of understanding in supporting stress- and trauma-affected people. These principles recognize the presence of trauma symptoms and acknowledge the role that trauma has and may continue to play.

- Trauma and stress result in adaptive behaviors that are expressed in response to negative experiences. These behaviors may be ineffective in a safe environment, and they are not under the direct control of the individual who has been affected.
- It is essential that stressed and traumatized people have safe physical and emotional environments, that their basic needs are met, and that their physical and social environments are consistent, predictable, and most of all respectful.
- Having relationships with people where respect, generosity, patience, and cooperation are displayed and authentic is essential to the development of understanding of the "non-

trauma" world. Such prosocial behaviors and attitudes are often unknown to those who are significantly affected by stress and trauma (Steele and Malchiodi, 2012).

One of the leading trauma-informed intervention frameworks is the Attachment, Self-Regulation, and Competency (ARC) model. This model identifies three core domains that often impact children, adolescents, and their families who experience trauma. This program has resulted in a reduction of post-trauma stress symptoms and anxiety as well as an increase in adaptive and social skills (Kinniburgh et al., 2005).

The ARC model's framework addresses issues affecting individual children as well as family functioning.

- **Attachment:** Strengthening attachment, especially with infants, involves helping adults to become aware of children's cues, respond to those cues appropriately, and establish consistent and predictable routines.
- **Self-regulation:** Helping children identify, manage, and appropriately express feelings and emotional states are the key elements in the self-regulation domain.
- **Competency:** Strengthening abilities in decision making, such as the ability to consider possible alternative actions, and developing self-awareness are focus points for the competence domain, as is the integration of trauma experiences. Integrating trauma experiences requires more skilled intervention with therapists or counselors.

One of the most valuable aspects of the ARC framework is its individualized application to a variety of caregiving settings, including early childhood programs and schools. There is no rigid protocol for its use, and the model continues to undergo development and refinement as it is implemented in numerous settings and programs throughout North America.

The behaviors of stress- and trauma-affected people are expressions of genuine need and are old patterns of response, inexperience, and distrust. Trauma-informed practices provide guidelines for mental and physical health professionals and educators to help people affected by stress and trauma to build permanent skills and perspectives. While used mostly in mental health settings, this approach can be extended into early childhood settings as well, helping children feel included, reducing sensory-physical impact, and increasing social and interpersonal skills.

Ideas for Practice

Respect is one of the most important feelings and experiences for children who encounter stress and trauma to have. Respect involves showing consideration for, appreciating, taking notice of, and valuing an individual. The following is a list of 10 everyday classroom practices that demonstrate respect for children. Match the everyday practice (list on page 51) with the quality of respect that is demonstrated in the practice.

QUALITIES OF RESPECT

A. Displaying courtesy
B. Validating personal expressions and feelings
C. Showing kindness and caretaking
D. Demonstrating fairness
E. Honoring the need for anticipating change
F. Supporting skills for knowing how to be included
G. Preserving dignity
H. Safeguarding privacy
I. Following through (keeping a promise)
J. Honoring feelings of security and being protected

CLASSROOM PRACTICES

_____ 1. When one of the children noticed that the birds could not find seeds to eat after a heavy snowfall, Teacher Steve asked the children what they might be able to do to help the birds. The children came up with a plan to make bird feeders and keep them filled.

_____ 2. Clay came to school angry and upset after a weekend visit with his father (his parents share custody and alternate weekend visitations). After talking with him about why he was upset (his father was going to be gone for his next visit), Teacher Lynn helped Clay write a short note to his father.

_____ 3. José was pleased to see his picture on the bulletin board when he came to kindergarten on Monday. On Friday, Teacher Michelle had said she would put it up, but José thought she was too busy to remember.

_____ 4. Mrs. Day's classroom has rules for being a part of the group and for feeling safe. One rule is that no one can push, shove, tease, hit, or shout at anyone else.

_____ 5. During the first week of Head Start, the children are told about the schedule for playing indoors and outdoors. The schedule is pictured on a big posted board, and Teacher Amy reminds the children to check the schedule board when they are not sure about what they will be doing next.

_____ 6. When behavior problems arise in Mr. Juarez's K–1 classroom, he speaks to the children privately and personally, not in front of other children.

_____ 7. Katerina's family places pride and value in her personal cleanliness and appearance. After a busy day in full-day preschool, Mrs. Pappas takes a few minutes to make sure Katerina's hands and face are clean and her clothes are tidy.

_____ 8. Ms. Williams tells Jaden, a new child in the classroom, about the rule for playing with the toys: "You can keep something until you are done playing with it; but, if you've stopped using it, then someone else can use it."

_____ 9. The children in Mr. Egan's class know their classroom saying: Everyone gets to [insert the activity], so we take turns and check to see who still needs to [name of activity].

_____ 10. Teachers Theresa and Justine ask all the children to use four "be kind to one another" phrases: _please, thank you, welcome,_ and _May I help?_

Key: 1 = C; 2 = B; 3 = I; 4 = J; 5 = E; 6 = H; 7 = G; 8 = F; 9 = D; 10 = A

Helping Them Heal

Approaches to Working with Children
Who Experience Stress and Trauma

FIVE THINGS WE KNOW

❶ Stress and trauma affect both the body and brain, negatively influencing physical and emotional responses and social and thinking skills.

❷ Long-term exposure to stress and trauma in childhood can have significant harmful outcomes for adult physical and mental health.

❸ Children ultimately respond to stress by developing and using coping strategies to regain a sense of balance; some strategies may be ineffective or unhealthy.

❹ A child's response to stress can be seen in unique combinations of physical, social-emotional, and cognitive behaviors, which may be difficult to identify as being stress induced.

❺ Trauma-informed care offers a way to better understand the cumulative impact of multiple stressors and how to focus programs and interventions to better meet the needs of stress- and trauma-affected people.

What Do Stressed Children Need?

All children who come to early childhood programs need to be with teachers

- who are genuinely responsive to their individual personalities and needs and maintain clear professional and personal boundaries;
- who provide warm, caring interpersonal interactions regardless of the behavior children display;
- who create and implement activities and experiences that are engaging, authentic, and appropriate for the children's abilities and skills;
- who create opportunities for children to play, especially outdoors, to have places to call their own, and to know they belong;
- who provide support for children's families and validate their cultures and life experiences;
- who collaborate with colleagues and display interest in their own growth as professionals; and
- who like and respect young children and childhood.

Children who experience stress and trauma, however, come to early childhood programs with vulnerabilities. These vulnerabilities result when children attempt to manage the overwhelming experiences, sensations, and feelings that come from being stressed and pushed beyond their ability to cope. Classroom strategies that support children and offset the impact of stress may be most effective if they focus on resilience and address children's unique strengths.

Increasing resiliency and feelings of self-efficacy are keys to providing effective support to children who experience stress. While it is impossible to end stress and trauma experiences for children outside the classroom, it is possible to equip them with some basic skills that can reduce the impact of stress and build new capabilities. Classroom practices that take advantage of children's existing strengths can help children build new skills for managing emotional responses and expanding self-sufficiency (Developing Child 2009; 2010).

Helping Them Heal

Understanding Resiliency and Protective Factors

Being resilient means a child is able to successfully adapt despite challenging or threatening circumstances (Steele and Malchiodi, 2012). The capacity of some children to rise above childhood experiences that are abusive, harsh, unstable, and negative has been well-documented. These unique qualities are present in most resilient children (Werner, 1984). These "hidden sources of strength" include the following:

- **A temperament that elicits positive responses from others, especially caring adults:** This characteristic also includes a tendency to play actively and seek out new experiences, have an optimistic outlook, and exhibit a sense of humor. Children with a resilient temperament (usually described as easygoing) are able to ask for help from adults or other children when needed.

- **An ability to interact in constructive social ways with other children and adults:** Resilient children display a strong capacity for self-reliance and independence, but not to the extent that they are isolated or exclusionary. This characteristic also includes the ability to engage in creative play and to know personal preferences and strengths.

- **A developing capacity to see alternate outcomes, to see problems from different points of view:** Children who believe there can be positive outcomes or at least positive parts to a negative situation fare better than those who are unable to take alternate perspectives to problems.

- **A close relationship with at least one caring adult (not necessarily a family member):** While this may seem a characteristic that is not really up to the child, this trait indicates the capacity for close connections and emotional responsiveness on a personal level. Having an affiliation with someone who the child knows is reliable and on the child's side is important for children able to overcome adversity (Breslin, 2005; Berson and Baggerly, 2009; Chu and Lieberman, 2010).

Classroom strategies that support children and offset the impact of stress may be most effective if they focus on resilience and address children's unique strengths.

Children's self-sufficiency and self-competence skills develop through a variety of supportive learning experiences. The more a child's self-competency skill set is developed, the more likely he will be able to favorably manage stress and its effects.

Protective Factors

While resiliency generally applies to individual characteristics that are present in and can be strengthened in children, other factors are important to offset the negative effects of adverse experiences. Protective factors are present in the external environment and interact with resiliency characteristics to provide an even stronger support system (Werner, 1990; Wolf, 2012). Protective factors may vary with the age of the child. For example, for a very young child, protective factors may include positive family communication and access to early health screenings. For a preschool and young school-age child, protective factors can include positive interactions with a small peer group (close friendships in the neighborhood or school) and opportunities to carry out meaningful tasks that provide nurturance and care for others. Protective factors exist within the child's immediate world (family and extended family) and in the neighborhood, especially in child care settings or school. Close, warm, and positive relationships with teachers can provide a significant source of protection for children who experience stress and trauma (Wolf, 2012).

Intervention and Prevention

Safe, stable, and nurturing experiences reduce the impact of stress for children, both in the short and long term. When planning such experiences for children, teachers must thoughtfully consider the strategies and approaches they will use. Some experiences that adults think are helpful may in fact be overwhelming, confusing, and more stress inducing than intended. In the mental health and public health fields, the focus on developing strategies and experiences for individuals at risk for negative life outcomes centers on the concepts of intervention and prevention (Blair and Raver, 2012; Kutash et al., 2006).

Intervention means acting in ways that may alter or prevent undesirable outcomes. For example, a child who can learn to calm herself at age four may be more likely to use this skill to diminish the feelings of anxiety that occur when a new (or repeated) stressor occurs in the future. Practices that help children reduce the physical sensations of stress may be considered intervention strategies.

The goal of intervention is to reduce the negative impact of stressful situations by changing the way an individual manages experiences so she may have better outcomes. Helping children to manage stress serves as an intervention to reduce the impact of inadequate coping strategies already developed. Developing new skills and abilities may help expand a child's options for a more positive future. Intervention strategies can also work to prevent further escalation of already existing negative experiences.

A strong partner to intervention, *prevention* focuses on building skills and understanding prior to the development of more negative responses. Simply put, prevention is focused on not developing poor behavior in the first place. Many of the practices that we use in early childhood classrooms have the potential to provide both intervention and prevention outcomes for children. For example, having a child clearly understand a consistent, predictable daily schedule in a preschool or kindergarten classroom may prevent that child from feeling lost, confused, or threatened. When children feel uncertain about what will happen next, they may act out, have difficulty with transitions, or withdraw from classroom routines and activities. Good classroom management is both a best practice and a prevention strategy.

Using intervention and prevention strategies can provide professionals with additional tools for making decisions about classroom practices. Many children come to school with feelings of tension and fear. Such feelings have little to do with their actual (reality-based) everyday classroom experiences. One way to decrease these physiological responses and lessen children's anxiety is to support observation skills that reveal the classroom for what it is: a place for playing, learning, being cared about, and making friends. By helping a child learn to see the classroom through guided observation coached by a caring teacher, the teacher can reduce a child's feelings of fear and tension. Optimally, the result will be an ability to see experiences with other children in a more positive way. Experiencing other children as positive—or at least not overwhelmingly fearful—can help children move away from using their past perspectives as their only option for understanding. New skills may prevent poor ones from developing further. For children, offsetting the impact of stress means regaining balance, self-sufficiency, and renewed interest. It means not feeling diminished, anxious, and afraid.

Children's Strengths

We know that high-quality early childhood experiences serve as significant protective factors for children who are at risk for negative outcomes. We also know that early childhood classroom teachers are a significant and important source of support and protection for young children. When early childhood programs can adapt to the needs of stressed children, children can benefit and thrive. Building protective, skill-strengthening, nurturing experiences for vulnerable children requires viewing children through a "strengths-based lens" (Fox, 2008).

Understanding children from a resiliency point of view means having the intention and capacity to see children's strengths as more important than their vulnerabilities. A strengths-based approach presumes that the child is doing the best she can and wants to be included, accepted, and make a contribution. This approach tries to identify areas of competency—no matter how small—"presuming the positive" about the child and her family (Hodas, 2006). To uncover and distinguish children's strengths, observe and ask thoughtful questions. Develop a sense of a child's unique assets by focusing on five areas of distinctiveness:

- activity favorites,
- sensory and environmental preferences,

- management of life routines,
- disposition, and
- learning style. (Fox, 2008; Katz, 2013; Dunn et al., 1993).

The following questions may be helpful in identifying children's individuality and strengths:

1. **What activities does he seem to prefer and enjoy?**
   Which does he choose frequently? Which ones does he avoid? Can he identify which activities he feels he is best at? Does he prefer outdoor, nature-focused activities or indoor building and block construction? Does he prefer writing, talking, reading alone or with others, exploring or being shown new materials by others, having visitors come to the classroom?

   Are you able to know his favorites from life outside school: foods, places to go, friends, family members, pets, toys, movies, clothes, books? What do you know about his neighborhood and living environment: house, apartment, mobile home, family income level, neighborhood conditions? Are there sidewalks, a yard, or streets for play? What are his experiences with transportation: family car, bus, subway or light rail? Are there other situations where he is in group care: afterschool; weekend child care; faith-based school or care; lessons in music, a second language, swimming, sports? Has he traveled out in the world beyond neighborhood, school, and community?

2. **Where and in what environment does he like to play?**
   What part of the room does he seem to prefer: tables, block corner, loft? outdoors or indoors? loud or quiet activities? Is he easily distracted by changes in light, temperature, or weather? How does he manage being crowded or left alone? Does he seem to have a best time of the day? What are his favorite play themes: pirates, superheroes, family? Does he prefer sitting, standing, moving around, or playing on the floor?

3. **How does he manage the routines of daily life?**
   Is he able to successfully handle eating, toileting, hand washing, tooth brushing, napping, managing personal

possessions, and coming and going from school? What
rituals and routines does he use? Are these social or solitary
activities? Is he comfortable with routines that involve daily
life tasks? Does he display any unusual habits? Is he tidy or
messy? Is he possessive or open about personal things, body
space, or being touched? Is going home easy, sometimes sad,
distressing, disorganized? How does he come to school, enter
the classroom, engage with other children and adults? Is he
sensitive to heat or cold? What time of day does he like to eat?

4. What is his disposition?

Is he curious, introspective, cautious, slow or quick to get
involved, easy or more challenging to talk with, open or slow
to engage in new experiences? Is he calm, excited, funny,
reserved, sneaky, reliable, consistent, fearful, spontaneous,
easily angered, reactive, sensitive, caring, shy, modest, noisy,
intrusive, watchful, patient, generous? Is he highly sensitive
to all sensory input or some more than others (Katz, 2013)? Is
he focused on or easily distracted from what he is doing? What
are his interaction preferences: small or large group, alone or
with close friends? What five words would you use to describe
the disposition of this child?

5. What is his learning preference?

There are two approaches that might be used to gain greater
understanding of a child's unique learning style or preferences.
(Bear in mind that children's learning styles are fluid and
changing: a child at five may appear to be a visual learner but
may develop into one who prefers reading and writing as these
skills emerge.) The first view of learning preferences is that of
understanding traditional learning styles. A second option is
to look at a child's intellectual preferences through the lens of
Howard Gardner's work on multiple intelligences.

A traditional view of learning styles describes four levels or
modalities: visual, auditory, read-write, and kinesthetic (Dunn
et al., 1993).

- **Visual mode:** The learner acquires understanding primarily
  through visual means and prefers to see information
  drawn out using maps, diagrams, images on paper with

words attached, drawings, or photographs. Doodling, making marks, and seeing the "real thing" are important to a visually dominant learner.

- **Auditory mode:** The learner has a preference for receiving information that is heard or spoken and learns best when information is verbally presented in small or large groups. In conversation, she may repeat what she has heard for clarification, may talk to herself to organize, and often talks through her process of understanding rather than sorting it out in her head first.

- **Read-write mode:** The learner prefers written information and needs to both read and then write information to understand it. While this mode of learning does not directly apply to children who are not yet able to read and write, it may develop quickly once children acquire these skills and provides an additional option for children to learn. An early indicator of this preference may be seen in kindergarten children who prefer to write stories and information once it has been presented orally or in text form.

- **Kinesthetic mode:** The learner prefers to learn through direct physical or perceptual interaction. Most preschool and kindergarten children have strong kinesthetic tendencies. Learning occurs most authentically and with greater ease for kinesthetic learners when they have direct interaction with the experience and information being presented. Demonstrations and opportunities for all senses to be involved (touch, taste, sound, sight, smell) are the most desirable ways for learning to occur. If kinesthetic learners are grounded in the experience of reality, they can then more easily use their physical understanding of the experience to move toward more abstract understandings.

Understanding learning styles presents opportunities for classroom design and instruction that may be a source of support for stressed children. Using a variety of methods to deliver information, especially information that concerns expectations for behaviors or schedules, transitions, and location of materials can be helpful to children with strong learning style preferences. A highly visual child, for example, is will be more receptive to information that comes to her in visual form and may be less aware of or receptive to information that is auditory. It is also possible that a child with a strong learning style may be more negatively influenced when stressors are delivered and received in the child's preferred style. A highly auditory child who repeatedly hears loud, angry arguments between his parents may find these events more stressful than a child who is strongly visual.

Gardner proposes that people organize, process, and understand their world through intellectual perspectives or intelligences. While people may use several of these areas of preference, most have one dominant learning approach. This area of preference and strength provides the most optimal window for learning and acquiring skills.

- **Bodily kinesthetic:** The learner uses body sensations to process information and express ideas and feelings. A bodily kinesthetic child moves or fidgets while sitting and standing; communicates through hands and gestures; mimics; learns by touching (including touching people); likes dramatic play, building and construction, creative movement, and physical activity; and often combines talking and action.

- **Social (combining interpersonal and intrapersonal intelligence):** The learner uses social interactions as a source of and way to process information and express ideas and feelings. A social learner generally talks easily and interacts with others; has strong friend groups; takes leadership roles including that of teaching or mentoring; is highly verbal and aware of social issues within a group, including attendance or names and characteristics of other children and adults; prefers working in groups (or in a quiet setting close to others) when learning new things; enjoys dramatic play, books, and oral stories. Note: A social learner may be either outgoing or more introverted and reserved.

- **Linguistic/Language:** The learner uses words, either oral or written, to process information and express ideas and feelings. A linguistic child has a strong preference for books and written materials; enjoys videos, games, rhymes, and funny stories; responds easily to verbal directions and information; may easily acquire a second language; has a strong vocabulary (if not highly verbal, uses descriptive vocabulary); communicates feelings well; and has a good memory.

- **Logical-Mathematical:** The learner uses symbols, especially numbers and patterns, to process information. A logical-mathematical child has a strong preference for playing games with rules and outcomes (checkers, chess) including computer games, enjoys discovering new things and recording the information and understanding how things work, prefers images and pictures to words, is very logical (versus emotional) in relating to others, organizes things in categories, and has a strong memory for the sequence of events and patterns.

- **Spatial:** The learner uses visual perception to process information and to express ideas and feelings. The spatial child

We also know that early childhood classroom teachers are a significant and important source of support and protection for young children.

has a strong preference for visual images (versus words); likes illustrations, pictures, videos, photographs, charts, and maps to locate place (versus written directions); generally has a good sense of direction and awareness of her body in space; can observe detail in visual images; may doodle when learning or listening; may prefer geometric puzzles, models, and patterns; is aware of color and color combinations; and may remember events by images versus social interaction.

- **Musical:** The learner uses rhythm, tone, and musical sounds (melody) to process information and to express ideas and feelings. The musical child may not be musically gifted but

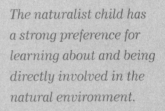

The naturalist child has a strong preference for learning about and being directly involved in the natural environment.

may prefer the auditory and kinesthetic blend that music provides for organizing and processing information. He will prefer to sing, hum, tap, or move in rhythm; respond emotionally to music; and use lyrics or sounds to express feelings or concepts. The musical child keeps music in his head, remembers musical sequences, assigns feelings to musical expressions, prefers music to the spoken word, may be sensitive to sound as a distraction, and has a strong memory for events where music is involved.

- **Naturalist:** The learner uses sensory characteristics of the natural world as a means to process information and express ideas and emotions. The naturalist child has a strong preference for learning about and being directly involved in the natural environment; likes direct interaction with living things, especially birds, animals, bugs, fish, and plants; may be interested in weather, stars and space, geology, and the forest or desert; collects and organizes things that are around the environment (man-made or natural); has strong memories for events that occur in outdoor spaces; is not bothered by being dirty; and may be uncomfortable in indoor, crowded environments.

Understanding intellectual preferences or learning styles can provide additional appreciation for how well some children have been able to manage difficult lives. Children's individual temperaments, dispositions for learning, skills, and personality characteristics—while not always best suited for life in traditional school settings—can be appreciated by those who can see past the worrisome behavior.

Developing a Strengths-Based Profile

One of the primary reasons for looking at children from a strengths-based perspective is to gain additional options for working with them based on their individual capabilities. Many early childhood and kindergarten programs focus on helping children increase skills in areas where assessment findings (either by formal evaluation or experienced observation) indicate concern. While this is important for strengthening emerging or below-norm skills, such a narrow focus risks overlooking children's unique areas of proficiency. This may be particularly true for children who may show deficits that are the result of stress effects.

Considering children's individuality and experiences as strengths can provide additional options for building competence. In a strengths-based view, characteristics, dispositions, and experiences can all be considered assets. Understanding and knowing a child's "environmental history" (Katz, 2013) is essential when identifying a child's strengths. Teachers and caregivers can use those unique characteristics to validate a child's identity and capabilities, regardless of negative or troublesome behaviors and problems. One way to compile what is known about a child from a strengths-based perspective is to look at three areas of development: learning strengths, relationships strengths, and experience strengths.

- Learning strengths include the ways in which a child approaches learning about the world: her sensory preferences, interests, use of symbols (letters/numbers, picture references), and responsiveness to new information and experiences.
- Relationship strengths include a child's skills and her approach to interacting with people, ways of expressing feelings, preferences for social-group inclusion and size, potential for social contribution, social awareness, and decision making in social settings.
- Experience strengths include skills, perspectives, and personal knowledge that the child has acquired through the process of living out in the world; ways of adapting and moving between different settings and situations; knowledge about the world; and a range of exposure to a diversity of people, animals, food, transportation, living conditions, and culture.

The following information and chart give an example of a strengths-based profile for a stressed child, with follow-up implications for practice.

Oscar

Oscar is four-and-a-half years old. He lives in a two-bedroom urban apartment with his younger sibling and his mom. Oscar's dad was arrested last year and is in prison for three to four years. Oscar walks to the bus with his mom, who drops him off at full-day preschool. After three months at school, this is what his teacher knows about him:

- He brings the same three to six food items for lunch daily, plays in the neighborhood park on the weekends near his grandma's apartment where he sometimes stays, has little experience outside his neighborhood, and must have adult supervision whenever he is out of the house.

- He prefers indoor play in the block area. He also likes to draw and color but is anxious about activities where he is asked to write letters or numbers. He is bilingual in English and Spanish, has three to five close friends at school, and is relatively uninterested in the other 14 children in the room. He is usually tidy in appearance and in how he manages eating, organizing personal things, and putting items away.

- Oscar is usually compliant with adult direction but may be disruptive when he is outdoors. He hits when in conflict with other children; sucks his first two fingers at various times during the day; and avoids dramatic play, movement activity and music, and circle-reading time unless the stories are about animals.

- He watches everything that goes on before making a decision to act and seems to be agitated when there is a great deal of random movement, action, and visual stimulation. He looks away or down when there is lots going on. When the class is on a field trip, he stays in the middle or the back of the group.

- He expresses interest (nonverbally, at first) in stories other children tell about pets, going to the zoo or the big park downtown, or events where police or fire personnel were involved. He likes to look at books about machines, trains, maps, and real-life situations.

TABLE 3A

Areas of Strength	Characteristics	Implications of Practice
Learning Strengths	■ Visual learning (drawing and blocks) and awareness seem strong ■ Prefers learning that is reality focused ■ Organized and sequential in his thinking ■ Prefers small groups for interaction	■ Provide information that is focused on real-life topics (not pretend, fantasy, or feelings focused) ■ Give visual information (versus auditory) ■ Small group (assume little learning takes place in large group) ■ Blend letter/number work with animals or machines topics and always in order/ sequence ■ Try sequence cards (instead of puzzles)
Relationship Strengths	■ Has formed close friendships and connections with a small group ■ Not distracted by the interactions around him ■ Cooperative, respectful, and responds to adult requests, especially indoors ■ Seems uncomfortable in large groups, especially when "creative display" is expected ■ Not a strong self-starter and social leader ■ Self-soothes with finger-sucking, especially when transitioning and not engaged ■ May have limited skills in verbal and social-interaction problem solving ■ Experienced loss and may not understand loss of connection to father	■ Use small group as his learning preference; being called out to perform in large group will be a stressor ■ Provide positive reinforcement for cooperation, especially when seen outdoors ■ Provide one or two rule-based activities for small group outdoors ■ Provide visual behavior cards to help with learning not to hit ■ Give touches or close personal verbal suggestions or support when finger sucking occurs ■ Provide clear visual evidence that his personal things are secure, he is a contributing part of the class and belongs there (not in large group format) Introduce "feelings" stories with animals as characters, without preachy overtones ■ Consider firefighter dramatic play themes and bring props into book area ■ Review diversity of pictures of men in the classroom and men invited as visitors

Areas of Strength	Characteristics	Implications of Practice
Experience strengths	■ Strong connections and familiarity with neighborhood ■ Manages transitions between settings well ■ Understands variety of adult roles and behaviors ■ Interested in opportunities and experiences that exist outside his immediate environment	■ Use experience of his neighborhood for drawings and creating a book (using his drawings) ■ Try small-group leadership role when on a short neighborhood walk ■ Make neighborhood maps (where children draw "places close to my house") ■ If possible, provide options for field trips to places where animals, machines/cars, or art (especially sculpture) may be available

Research and best practice have focused on strengthening children's resilience and understanding intervention and prevention as ways to help children impacted by stress and trauma. We know that children who are stressed and experience trauma come to early childhood settings with challenging behaviors, feelings, and ways of understanding people and events. These children are the recipients of continued "high environmental loads" and often harsh and unpredictable "environmental histories" (Greenman, 2007; Katz, 2013). Helping stress-vulnerable children requires an understanding of the impact of common classroom practices as well as an awareness of developing special experiences to meet their needs. By understanding each child's unique strength profile, teachers can identify and create classroom practices that build strength, resilience, and self-competence.

Ideas for Practice

Look at each item in the following list, and place it on the chart. All of these activities and experiences can build skills that foster resiliency.

Strategy	Classroom Practice
Constructing a sense of community	
Regulating body-sensory responses	
Building self-competence skills	

1. Having an identified place for personal possessions
2. Having a class name or identity
3. Experiencing visitors to the classroom who demonstrate skills, play music, or prepare food
4. Drawing life-size body outlines
5. Having a predictable daily schedule
6. Celebrating special occasions (not necessarily traditional holidays)
7. Participating in dramatic play where themes may be about favorite stories or events
8. Having responsibility for classroom chores and helping others
9. Being exposed to books and stories about feelings and overcoming problems
10. Having a designated daily time for rest and quiet
11. Being able to recite short, funny, or clever poems
12. Playing variations on Simon Says—moving fast, walking backward, jumping, and so on

Helping Them Heal

Creating a
Sense of
Community

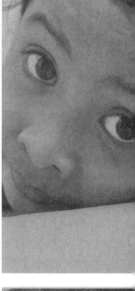

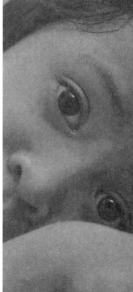

FIVE THINGS WE KNOW

❶ All children have learning, relationship, and experiential strengths that can be developed to increase their resiliency skills.

❷ One way to understand the effects of stress and trauma on children is to remember that they experience the world through three filters: sensory-physical, social-emotional, and thinking-understanding.

❸ Everyday experiences, as well as those specifically focused on supporting children's vulnerabilities, can reduce the negative effects of stress.

❹ For children who experience stress and trauma, it is essential that they feel that their classrooms are safe, stable, and nurturing places.

❺ If adults accept children's behavior and coping strategies as a reflection of the children's inexperience and vulnerabilities, then understanding and patience are much easier.

What Is Classroom Community?

For most of us, the word *community* refers to a group of people who live in the same area or share common interests or experiences, a place where people have goals and life experiences in common. Belonging to a community is an essential part of the human social experience. As children, we learn the routines and expectations of the multiple cultures and communities in which we live. We encounter both positive, affirming experiences as well as those that may be less desirable. Early childhood programs, schools, and classrooms are central to children's understanding of belonging with others and what it means to be valued and connected (Riley et al., 2008).

Child care centers, homes, and schools are microcommunities that reflect adult beliefs in children's capacities to grow and learn. Hopefully these places are welcoming; provide a sense of organization, purpose, and quality; reflect the personalities and values of the children, teachers, and their families; and are places where their inhabitants want to go and are accepted. A classroom that builds and sustains a sense of place and community should reflect a spirit of acceptance, caring, and predictability (Stone, 2001).

A quality classroom community provides the foundation upon which more specific interventions and practices can be implemented. Everyday stress experiences that occur in a typical classroom provide a way for children to acquire resilience and a greater capacity for engaging with others; however, when a child perceives the classroom as a place of overwhelming tensions, even well-intended experiences can become overly stressful (Berson and Baggerly, 2009).

Being part of a community, especially a classroom community, often comes with expectations for making a contribution. Expectations for helping out and being kind are all potential social-skill outcomes of community connection. Making an authentic contribution to others can help children feel validated, important, and competent as individuals (Epstein, 2011). Children can also extend their understanding of community through involvement in field trips or service for others outside the classroom, such as recycling, writing letters, holding food drives, and so on.

A classroom community and culture that assists children who are stressed and vulnerable is one where the physical environment and classroom organization become part of the children's protection and support system. Providing a quality environment is a way to develop more authentic connections with stressed children. Intentionally choose to limit children's exposure to commercial and adult-focused culture that dominates outside of early childhood and kindergarten classrooms (Katz and McClellan, 1991; Kostelnik et al., 2011).

DEFINING HEALING

The idea of healing has many definitions and understandings, from the physical to the spiritual. For many people, *healing* means "to mend or cure" (back to where I was, and nothing has changed) or "to regain a sense of balance" (a feeling of wholeness—but maybe not the same as before). Early childhood caregivers may foster healing in children who have experienced stress and, especially, trauma by helping them to learn new skills and ideas that will provide balance and strength; by offering small, quiet, peaceful experiences as alternatives to threat and anxiety; and by providing an environment where children can build authentic connections to people who can be trusted.

Elements of a Safe Classroom

Begin creating a classroom that provides a safe environment by looking at the physical environment, the routines, and the experiences that build connections to others. To know they are safe, children must be able to easily identify the following characteristics:

- The classroom is physically and emotionally free from threat, fear, and uncertainty.
- The classroom and routine have order and reasonable predictability.

- The activities encourage connection to others.
- The activities offer opportunities for interesting and authentic learning.

A safe, nurturing classroom community builds memorable, positive experiences that are unique to the individuals who live in the space. Create memories and stories that result in personal histories: celebrations; ways of interacting and connecting with one another; rituals; ways of honoring people outside classroom life; support for changes we know are coming, such as field trips, visits to clinics or the dentist, long weekends away from school, or moving to a new home; even ways of dressing, eating, and keeping records of events (Honig, 2009; Katz, 2013; Kostelnik et al., 2011).

How Does Physical Space Affect Children?

Child care programs and schools are places where children live for a large portion of the day. The quality of the physical environment can support their development or add to levels of stress and reactivity. Children experience space and place differently and with greater meaning than adults do (Greenman, 2007).

For children, especially young children, sensory experiences can provide critical information, welcoming images of connection, warnings of danger, and will affect mood and choice of behavior (Greenman, 2007). For a child's developing brain, however, processing and organizing the complexity and intensity of sensory data is often overwhelming and exhausting. Unfortunately, intense, disorganized, and anxiety-producing experiences are the "norm" for stressed and traumatized children (Arnold and Fisch, 2011). They need physical places where predictability, opportunity for self-reliance, lower environmental load, and low-risk connection with others are the priorities.

Greenman describes *environmental load* as how the complexity, familiarity, flow, and intensity of environmental stimuli affect behavior and feelings. Places with high environmental load, such as a crowded urban street or apartment, the airport, or a shopping mall, involve lots of stimuli—noises, sights, smells, movement—that result in intense physiological responses of fear, anxiety, or excitement. These high levels of intensity can only be endured for limited periods of time. For children, repeated exposure to high environmental-load experiences produces chronic stress reactions.

A safe, nurturing classroom community builds memorable, positive experiences that are unique to the individuals who live in the space.

Places with lower environmental loads, such as reading rooms in libraries, quiet outdoor parks, organized play rooms, or bedrooms, provide predictable, moderated stimulation with less multisensory impact. Children may seek out stimulation in some of these low-load places, but they will do so by choice rather than reacting to a stimulus. In more organized and less stimulating environments, children are much better able to calm themselves, attend carefully to new experiences, and regain a sense of balance.

One of the many ways children know they are a part of a social group is by how the physical space is organized and inhabited. The following sections include checklists that focus on important parts of classroom community and space:
- organization and use of physical space,
- sensory environment, and
- building social connections.

Each is a starting point for looking at the ways children, especially stressed children, may experience spaces in early childhood programs.

Organization and Use of Physical Space

We know that children are strongly affected by how their environment is organized. While they are most focused on what is immediately at hand, they also learn to adapt and function within physical space. Placement of physical objects, furniture, pathways, and access to different areas all require that children adapt and change their awareness and behavior. The physical qualities of the space provide cues and specific information as to how children should behave, connect to and treat others, and directs how their learning takes place.

for children who experience stress and trauma, having to negotiate an intense and disorganized physical space—especially when they spend significant amounts of time in that space—can become an additional stressor. Predictability in schedule, location of objects and information, and clear expectations about what to do serve as points of stability and may be in stark contrast to their lives outside the classroom.

PRIVACY AND POSSESSIONS

Children who experience stress and trauma have widely varying encounters with loss, privacy, and invasion of their personal space. Some have had little experience in understanding the idea of common, shared space and possessions in a group setting. They may have a difficult time sharing, maintaining physical space boundaries, and being in close proximity to other children. Extra attention and coaching may help these children learn to negotiate the subtle rules of personal space. Loss of possessions is also common for children who experience stress and trauma. As a result, they are often highly protective of things they do have, are suspicious of the sharing expectation, worry about what other children are doing, or may be very disrespectful of another's work and possessions. Providing a means to ensure children that their personal possessions and projects are respected and protected is important. Being tolerant and understanding of their apprehension can, over time, reduce their possessiveness and anxiety.

Consider children's experiences with the organization and use of space. Does the classroom community provide the following?

- clearly defined areas for social gathering in groups of two or three people, small groups, and large groups
- clearly defined places where people enter and exit and where private interactions of greeting and departure can occur
- storage of personal property
- authentically useful, current, and understandable visual information on walls, doors, and so on
- wall spaces that are organized and not visually overwhelming
- windows free of clutter and pictures so the outside is visible, even at a glance

- clear, understandable displays of information about where to go and what to do in an emergency
- easily visible representations of children's and families' home languages and cultures
- furnishings that are organized to encourage focus and discourage running and more disruptive behavior
- materials that are organized and easily accessible

- space for quiet alone time but visible to the teacher at all times
- clear identification of cubbie, locker, and storage spaces where names are clearly and accurately printed
- practice and experience in moving to and from different classrooms within the same building so children are comfortable within their larger school space
- practice moving between inside and outside learning and play spaces
- a predictable schedule (in picture and written form) for when children are expected to be in different locations and engaged in different activities and behaviors
- transition strategies, such as visual prompts, communication books, sequence strips, simple signals, timers, and options for

"what to do when not everyone is ready" (Thelen and Klifman, 2011)

- visual cues that help children remember rules for different kinds of activity and use of space, such as the bathroom, free choice time, small group activities, snack and meal times, reading and circle time, and so on

Sensory Environment

Every classroom has a distinctive sensory "footprint." Can you remember what your first-grade classroom smelled like or that it had a particular feeling about it? These memories form as children spend extended periods of time in classrooms where they share experiences with others and interact on a very personal, sensory level with the physical layout. One way of supporting a child's sensory-physical filter so that it provides reasonably accurate and balanced images of what children encounter is to evaluate how children experience the environment through vision, hearing, touch, and smell.

Use the questions below to review the sensory impact of the physical space in a classroom. Consider children's visual experiences. Does the classroom community provide

- an overall physical environment that is a place of calm, order, interest, and restoration?
- at least two different sources of light, both artificial and natural?
- an opportunity for children to sit quietly alone or in small groups in a space where natural light is present at least once a day?
- large areas of nonprimary colors, such as muted natural tones of beige, cream, tan, and soft green or soft shades of amber, orange, purple, green, magenta, and chartreuse?
- a defined place of visual calm in pastel or muted colors, without interference from calendars, signs, alphabet and number charts, lists of rules, and other sources of information that require attention?
- places designated for organized display, both on walls and on surface areas, of children's work; objects related to an experience, such as items from a field trip; art and creative

expression; photographs on a related theme; 3-D construction; or project work?

- visual materials created by the children and teachers, rather than commercially produced visual materials such as super heroes, exaggerated animal and human figures, and television characters?
- consistency in the use of symbols throughout the classroom and in calendars and information posters?
- access to a quiet thinking space where colors and pictures offer a calming, peaceful scene (even on the ceiling)?
- the occasional opportunity for discovery and surprise, such as a surprise box or a scrapbook prepared by the teacher?
- pictures and drawings that accurately reflect the diversity of children and families in the program or school?
- a place where aesthetics—the experience of color, light, art, design, and place—are a priority?

Every classroom has a distinctive sensory "footprint."

Consider children's auditory experiences. Does the classroom community provide

- times when sound throughout the entire classroom space is consistent; for example, the whole space is quiet or busy with voices and activity or filled with soothing music or nature sounds?
- opportunity for exclusive, individual use of head phones for noise reduction and/or listening?

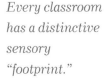

Creating a Sense of Community   **79**

- expectations for all children and adults to use quiet voices indoors?
- experiences with music and sound that teach the concepts of tone, volume, pitch, intensity, loud/soft, fast/slow, and soothing/active?
- opportunities for playing or making music and sounds that are moderated and controlled, such as ringing small bells, using soft sticks for drumming, or chanting in a small group?
- options for using auditory cues when making transitions; for example, ringing bells for going outside or playing a small gong for getting ready for lunch?
- opportunities to hear a variety of human voices reading, conversing, singing, and chanting, both live and recorded?
- orientation to warning sounds that are used for fire drills, evacuation, and so on, given prior to events?
- experiences where children practice listening to conversation, sounds, and recorded stories?

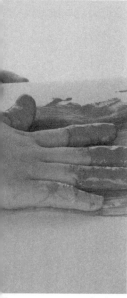

Consider children's kinesthetic experiences. Does the classroom community provide

- a variety of options for hands-on connection to textures, both in activities and throughout the classroom?
- opportunities to engage with living things, including plants, birds, and animals, and to have direct "touch-time" with these living things?
- daily experiences with fine and gross motor exercise, practice, and creative expression?
- experiences with movement and dance using live and recorded music, both lyrical and rhythmic?
- opportunity for rest or relaxation time on soft and comforting mats or resting surfaces?
- arrangement of furnishings and traffic flow that minimizes bumping into objects so children can easily move through spaces?
- clear, easily understood natural or created boundaries between defined spaces, learning centers, exits and entrances, storage areas, bathrooms, and so on?

Consider children's olfactory experiences. Does the classroom community provide

- well-ventilated classroom, bathroom, and other shared indoor spaces?
- limited interactions with people wearing strong perfume or detergent/fabric softener scents?
- options for children who are highly sensitive to cigarette smoke to be placed away from those who may have this smell in their clothes or hair?
- opportunities to discuss smell and one's personal likes and dislikes as part of the curriculum?
- experiences in identifying a variety of smells, from the familiar to the unusual?
- experiences with natural, soothing smells (not artificial air fresheners) during rest or relaxation times? (Safety note: Keep essential oils out of the reach of children.)
- opportunities to experience outdoor air at least twice daily, with time for a few minutes of deep breathing?

Building Connections

One of the critical elements of community is having connections to others, especially having associations and relationships that offer a variety of experiences. We need people who provide support, nurturance, friendship, joy and humor, sympathy, stories, inspiration, and intellectual challenge. Before children can develop more significant relationships, they need repeated positive interactions with those around them. It takes time to build relationships, and the inexperience and immature social skills of most children can make this process more difficult (Katz, 2013; Stone, 2001).

Building a network of extended or secondary connections to others expands children's chances to engage successfully with people, to learn more about how people live and behave, and how others may differ from familiar people. Extended connections are those where the person may not be directly present or may be absent for a time.

A note on smell: Smell and memory of scent is one of the longest lasting sensory impressions that people experience. Because stress and trauma are multisensory experiences, smell is often associated with negative events. Scent memories can sometimes be triggers for anxiety and fear even when experienced in settings unrelated to the initial stressor. Helping children build an inventory of smells by introducing scents associated with peaceful and calming experiences can provide alternatives for children who associate smells with stress or trauma.

We know children are very immediate and present in the moment, and these secondary connections may expand their understanding of time and place as well as their inventory of "people I know about."

Building real and secondary connections to people is important for children affected by stress and trauma. Their experiences with people may be sources of anxiety and mistrust, causing these emotions to dominate their understanding. They may have exposure to a limited range of people and may be unskilled in making even the most basic of emotional and social connections. Making close and informal connections to people builds emotional and social resilience. The skills developed in connecting with others are critical for improving the lives and learning potential of children affected by stress and trauma (Riley et al., 2008; Summers and Chazan-Cohen, 2012). Making connections with others requires three things:

RITUALS AND ROUTINES

Rituals are a set of special behaviors that are repeated over time and have personal and social meaning to a group of people. Rituals provide us with a sense of identity and belonging, assist in life transitions, and are often the source of shared memory and experience.

Routines are organized, frequently repeated behaviors that lack the symbolic or emotional meaning of rituals. Routines are always performed in a series of steps and are part of getting on with the business of life: preparing for mealtimes, getting ready for and going to school, and picking up classrooms. While little thought generally goes into routines once established, changes and major revisions require significant adaptation, especially for children.

Blending ritual practices with ordinary routines can provide children with a sense of continuity, partnership, and security. Involvement in daily routines and rituals helps children learn the rules and expectations of working and interacting with others, providing opportunities for important shared social experiences and ways for children to know the expectations for their involvement (Gillespie and Petersen, 2012).

- repeated opportunities,
- understanding that one is part of and contributes to a group, and
- sustaining linkages over time.

Participation (even if it is just observing) in rituals, routines, celebrations, keeping memories, having responsibilities, and being a friend are essential building blocks for becoming connected (Thelen and Klifman, 2011). The questions below can provide teachers with ideas for initiating and sustaining a culture of connection (Curtis and Carter, 2003) for children in classroom settings.

Consider children's experiences for making connections to others. Does the classroom community provide

- daily rituals for being greeted and saying goodbye? Do adults get down on the child's level and have warm, personalized interactions, which may include appropriate touch?
- the possibility for new children to have a buddy or mentor to assist with transition and orientation to the classroom?
- an identity for the classroom, such as a class name; chant, pledge, or song; flag or symbol; or webpage?
- opportunities to participate in celebrations, both the traditional and those that are unique to the classroom?
- clarification and practice of rituals for celebrations and special occasions; for example, name tags for field trips, singing a special song for birthdays, or saying *hip-hip-hooray* when a good event happens?
- opportunities to visit and bring a gift to other classrooms in the same building or others close by, to learn about the children in that room?
- opportunities for being mentors or email/pen-pal friends with other children?
- long-term volunteers in the classroom, such as a class grandmother or grandfather, reading partners, outdoor play monitor and coach, weekly special baker, language tutor, and so on?
- options to make connections to people or other groups of children in the community, such as email pals in another city, older people in a care facility, or an expert who has an interesting job who can chat with them over time?

- time to interview and meet with other people in the building who are not directly involved in the classroom, such as the director or principal, custodian, cook, or secretary?
- daily taking of attendance and a brief discussion of who is and is not present? If someone in the classroom community (including adults) is absent for two or three days, is an email or note sent to that person?
- easy identification of each child's name throughout the classroom on her cubbie, placemat, chair, circle mat, coat hook, and so on?
- a special space where artifacts and family objects are displayed and kept safe, such as a family picture wall, "show and see" box, display board, or tabletop, and including an easily read explanation about the display and family? (Curtis and Carter, 2003)
- a process for recording memories for the classroom and individual children, such as photographs or videos; scrapbooks; personal journals; notices of special occasions, visitors, or field trips; and portfolios? Are pictures sent home and kept at school for safekeeping? Are these memory books occasionally reviewed with the children, especially when they leave the program?
- opportunities for children to use cameras for recording classroom events, friends, and favorite things?
- expectations for genuine caring for other living and valued things, including plants, animals, special toys and equipment, visitors, newcomers to the classroom, and special displays?

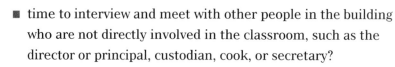

THE ART OF MAKING A FRIEND

Connecting with others means being able to establish a social link. Building these associations requires that people communicate both verbally and nonverbally in ways that invite others to join in the connection. For children, these associations are usually through collaborative play as playmates or as members of a familiar social group. Building these important connections requires skill in listening and responding.

For children who are stressed, these reflective abilities—paying attention and being present in the moment—may be more difficult to achieve. One way to help all children in the classroom is to practice the art of making a friend. By coaching children to follow the guidelines for connecting, you can increase their opportunities for being with others:

In our classroom,

- we pay careful attention when someone is talking, and we listen to what the person is saying;
- remember that we can say things with words and touch; and
- remember to follow through, to do what we said we would.
  (Hendrick, 2003)

- possibility for an "adopted" animal friend to visit, read with children, or function as a therapy pet?
- an expectation for each child to make a contribution, such as attendance taker, door holder, table setter, lunch helper, safety monitor, outside time keeper, and book collector?

Early childhood experiences can provide an alternative to a child's life outside the classroom, offering healing and restoration. A classroom community that reflects the key elements of clearly defined spaces, quality interactions with adults and other children, engagement in rituals and routines with clear expectations, and opportunities for improving social skills and acquiring new

learning can provide the base from which stressed children gain strength and even heal.

The flexibility inherent in early childhood programs provides the perfect opportunity for teachers and administrators to revisit their priorities and options for supporting the needs of stressed children. Early childhood classrooms should always be safe places for children. Reviewing how the organization, layout and use of physical space, sensory environment, and systems used to help children make connections can help identify important elements of creating a warm, intentional, interesting, and healing classroom community.

Ideas for Practice

In 1992 Lilian Katz wrote one of her most significant papers, which addressed assessing quality in early childhood programs. She offers four ways to view quality in early childhood classrooms:

- taking a *top-down perspective,* which reviews meeting licensing and other basic criteria for adult-child ratios, hygiene, square footage, and working conditions;
- taking an *outside-inside perspective,* which considers family perspectives of relationships, interactions with staff, and program or school values and goals;
- taking the *inside-outside perspective,* which looks at staff's personal feelings about work climate, administrative and colleague support, and long-term commitment; and
- taking the *bottom-up perspective,* which focuses on quality from the child's point of view and experience.

Early childhood classrooms should always be safe places for children.

The bottom-up view considers the questions on the following list. The term *experience* is broadly used and includes informal social interactions, time in free choice and small groups, lunch and transition times, outdoor/recess time, and the general tone or climate of the classroom. Look at your classroom from the perspective of the children, and answer these questions:

- Do I usually feel welcome in this environment?
- Do I feel I belong, rather than as just one of the crowd?
- Do I feel accepted, understood, and protected, rather than scolded or neglected by adults?
- Am I usually accepted by the majority of my peers?
- Am I usually addressed seriously and respectfully, rather than as "cute" or "precious"?
- Do I find most activities and lessons engaging, absorbing, and challenging, rather than just amusing, fun, entertaining, or exciting?
- Do I find most experiences interesting, rather than frivolous or boring?
- Do I find most activities meaningful, rather than mindless or trivial?

- Do I find most experiences satisfying, rather than frustrating or confusing?
- Am I usually glad to be here, rather than eager to leave?

Building

Self-Regulation Skills

FIVE THINGS WE KNOW

❶ The three experience filters—sensory-physical, social-emotional, and thinking-understanding—play a major role in determining how children physically and emotionally respond to stress.

❷ In the ARC trauma-informed care model (Kinniburgh et al., 2005), strengthening self-regulation and competence are most helpful for children.

❸ It is essential that children who experience stress and trauma feel they are able to manage their own feelings and reactions to the world around them.

❹ For children who experience stress and trauma, feeling and knowing they are part of a classroom community is essential to strengthening their resiliency skills.

❺ Building a sense of classroom community through attention to the physical and social environment lays the foundation for more focused skill development.

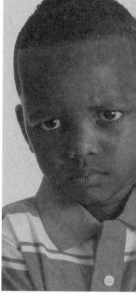

Understanding
Children's Responses

We know that children adopt coping strategies in response to stress and trauma as a means of managing and attempting to reduce the physiological and emotional impact of stress. Some of these coping strategies are not necessarily helpful in getting children what they may ultimately want and need: to decrease negative feelings and to increase feelings of personal safety and connection to others.

Stress responses are influenced by such factors as individual temperament, age, and developmental ability; the type, severity, duration, and chronic or acute nature of stress; the child's areas of strength as well as vulnerability; and the amount of external social and emotional support the child receives (Developing Child, 2011; Hodas, 2006; Katz, 2013; Summers and Chazen-Cohen, 2012). Early childhood professionals who recognize the need to respect a child's experiences with stress and trauma should consider how they might provide options to decrease negative behavior and develop new skills (Hodas, 2006).

Trying to respond to the varying types and intensity of children's stress-affected behavior can be daunting. Where should a caregiver start? One child, for example, may be out of control. Another may be anxious and afraid. Yet another may seem fine but may have a few very bad days. Just being aware of the kinds of behaviors associated with stress and trauma is a good beginning. Understanding how the child has come to cope with stressors adds another piece to the puzzle.

One way professionals describe different types of reactions children exhibit is to categorize them into two broad groups of symptoms and behaviors (Hodas, 2006; Summers and Chazen-Cohen, 2012):

- **Internalized Symptoms:** Internalized symptoms reflect feelings and behaviors that are directed inward.
    - problems with sleep, including nightmares
    - problems with eating

- withdrawal and self-imposed isolation
- anxiety and persistent worrying
- hypervigilance
- lack of attention, especially in social groups
- general fearfulness
- general complaints about body aches and pains
- regressive behaviors such as thumb sucking, bedwetting, and irrational fears (especially of the dark and/or monsters)
- crying and whimpering
- minor compulsive or ritualistic behaviors about everyday management of clothing, food selection, eating, schedules, or possession of toys
- inability to become calm in nonstressed situations

- **Externalized Symptoms:** Externalized symptoms are behaviors that are directed outward.
  - acting out aggressively, both spontaneously and intentionally
  - being irritable and reactive
  - being noncompliant with routine requests
  - engaging in disruptive behavior with others and with the general classroom community
  - lying and being overtly socially manipulative
  - showing strong reactions to sharing, taking turns, and winning and losing

It is not uncommon for children to show both kinds of symptoms, especially when expressions of externalized behaviors occur. Both patterns of behavior reflect the physiological process that is a child's response to stress and trauma. Regardless of whether a child is displaying externalized or internalized behaviors and emotions, there are three elements in common:

1. A stressed child is filled with intense emotions he may not, and usually does not, recognize.
2. A stressed child has developed long-standing physical habits of responding to being stressed and to stress triggers.
3. These behaviors are likely to continue unless the child is able to adopt alternative behaviors and learn to better manage his physical reactions (Hodas, 2006; Katz, 2013; Steele and Malchiodi, 2012).

Helping Children Manage the Impact of Stress Symptoms

Considering the complexity and range of behaviors that children express in reaction to stress, deciding upon a single approach is not only unreasonable but also highly unlikely to be effective (Blaustein and Kinniburgh, 2010; Katz, 2013; Steele and Malchiodi, 2012). Stressed children need to strengthen their capacities for self-regulation, which can lead to a decrease in stress- and hormone-induced behaviors and reduction in the old ways of

coping. If new options are made available and practiced with the children, they will increase children's cognitive processing skills. To learn high-order cognitive processing skills, stressed children must first be able to manage their responses to the sensory stimuli within their environment (Bredekamp, 2010).

The ability to self-regulate applies to many areas of development: emotional, behavioral, physical, and even cognitive. This complex ability develops slowly and is dependent on direction and learning provided from the external environment (Florez, 2011). Physical feelings and reactions are directly tied to emotional and behavioral responses; being able to manage them lays the groundwork for developing more complex, cognitively linked skills. Florez notes that emotional and cognitive self-regulation are not separate; emotional regulation affects cognitive functioning and vice versa. Helping children modify response and pay attention to the details of the senses is the starting point for building common ground in self-regulation.

One of the most important findings of brain-based research has been the identification of a set of intellectual skills known as *executive functioning* (Developing Child, 2012b; Katz, 2013). Executive functioning refers to the ability to process information and manage oneself in order to achieve a goal; for example, Jett is five years old and may use his executive skills to think, "I need to finish reading time with the group, and then I can go outside." These skills are neurologically based and involve working memory (what is going on right now and what happened in the recent past), mental flexibility (being able to think of multiple ways of doing something or solutions), and self-control (ability to demonstrate awareness, attention, and restraint). This diverse and complex set of skills is essential for developing building blocks for school achievement, constructive and positive interactions with others, personal achievement, and the management of life's challenges and stress.

Executive functioning refers to the ability to process information and manage oneself in order to achieve a goal.

Understanding Self-Regulation

Gillespie and Seibel (2006) define *self-regulation* as a child's ability to gain control of bodily functions, manage powerful emotions, maintain focus and attention, and ultimately make thoughtful decisions. Self-regulation involves managing one's emotional responses, inhibiting strong reactions from dominating decision making, and gaining increasing skills in identifying and responding appropriately to the emotions and behaviors of others (Epstein, 2011; Gartrell, 2012; Pizzolongo and Hunter, 2011).

Self-regulation develops as a process of maturation and through opportunities to learn from other children and calm, thoughtful, intentional adults. Many children who experience stress and trauma remain somewhat hypersensitive to stress triggers and general conditions of stress. While their behavior may appear intentional, especially for preschool and kindergarten-aged children, it is more likely that it is reactive, impulsive, and the result of limited social and emotional competence, emotional immaturity, and/or physiological factors (Hodas, 2006; Marion, 2011). To help children better manage emotions and stress responses, provide a calm, organized, and predictable environment. Appropriate classroom practices, especially those focused on sensory regulation, can become the physical and emotional safety net needed to increase the opportunity for constructive functioning (Gartrell, 2012; Hodas, 2006).

A child's unique physiological makeup will influence how she responds to everyday events as well as stress experiences. Often when we talk about self-regulation, the focus is on high-profile children who consistently seem overly sensitive and reactive. However, a display of overly reactive behavior may result from a lack of awareness and sensitivity to subtle social and emotional cues. Not only do children need to manage strong emotional responses but they also need to learn what to do in order to move forward (Gartrell, 2012). Provide children with models, techniques, and skills that can help them modify their intense responses so they can begin to recognize and understand subtle experiences and cues. Helping children reduce intense reactions, both internalized and externalized, means knowing the level of reactivity and sensitivity each child has in response to sensory stimuli. Sensory regulation is the ability to receive, organize, understand, and then adapt in response to the sensory data (Katz, 2013).

As children develop and gain experience with sensory information, they are able to build their understanding about the experiences in which they participate. They become able to communicate more effectively about what they have seen, heard, tasted, smelled, or touched and can let others know about their preferences and feelings. The "mixing together" of sensory information is dependent on two others factors: sensitivity and reactivity (Katz, 2013). *Sensitivity* refers to a person's threshold or receptiveness to the strength of sensory data. In other words, how strong is a person's awareness? For example, how aware is he of noise level? How attuned is she to differences in taste, texture, and temperature of food? How sensitive is he to movement, light, or temperature change in a room? *Reactivity* refers to the level of response to sensory data. Katz notes that reactivity refers to what the person does in response to sensory input. Not unlike sensitivity, reactivity comes in degrees of reaction: high reactivity can involve jerking away or hitting; low reactivity can involve ignoring but being aware of a sensation, moving away, or adjusting to be more comfortable.

Children may be highly sensitive and highly reactive, or they may be highly sensitive but have lower reactivity. Sensory processing and adapting are the keys to understanding the varying degrees or levels of intensity that children express in response to sensory experiences (Katz, 2013). It stands to reason that children who experience high levels of sensory sensitivity are more likely to have strong reactions to the intense experiences of stress.

Kasey

Kasey just transferred midyear to a new kindergarten classroom of 20 other children. This is her third transfer this year. Her new teacher, Ms. Jackson, has noticed that she seems easily distracted by the activities of other children who are close by and pays close attention to conversations between teachers and other adults. She frequently chews on pencils, her hair, and the insides of her mouth, especially when she is trying to attend to a task that requires her to work on her own with other children in close proximity. Ms. Jackson is concerned that Kasey is highly sensitive to noise, especially the sounds generated by social conversation, and finds it very difficult to desensitize this type of sensory input and concentrate on tasks by herself. Her calming behaviors may be mechanisms to reduce the intensity of the auditory sensory information. While she may be sensitive to these types of sounds, she is not overly reactive to them.

Ms. Jackson asks Kasey if she would like to work in a corner of the room where there are fewer conversations and noise distractions. She also asks the other adults working with the children to speak more quietly, especially during work time and when they are in close proximity to Kasey. Ms. Jackson does see a reduction in Kasey's chewing behavior during work time. The behavior continues to be a part of her coping system, however, especially when she is in large group time where there are lots of conversations and interaction.

TOUCH

Touch is one of the most important of human needs. Having experiences with positive and comforting touch is also one very important way for children who experience stress and trauma to find comfort, reassurance, validation, and healing. Frances Carlson notes that children with low touch experience have higher rates of violent behavior because they have learned that the only way to be in physical contact is through aggressive interactions. The role early childhood professionals play in providing experiences with positive touch and physical contact is an important one. As mature adults who value the integrity of dependent children, teachers know that daily experiences with touch, such as a hand on a child's back, shoulder, knee, or arm; a high five and "well done" handshake; holding hands; and a warm hug can make a significant difference. With careful considerations for children's individual and cultural needs, the therapeutic value of touch provides the best benefit children can receive: that of feeling and being connected.

Modifying Children's Responses to Stress

We can help children modify their reactions to stress and undo some old patterns by providing multiple options for calming the body, increasing familiarity with nonthreatening sensory experiences, and providing alternatives for the brain to process these types of experiences. Of equal importance is the development of a more in-control image of self. Gartrell proposes that a significant side-effect of stress and trauma is the self-fulfilling expectation of rejection based on a child's emerging negative self-image. The greater a child's capacity to manage and regulate how she responds to stress-related stimuli, the greater the feeling of self-efficacy and the sense that she can do something about how a stimulus feels to her—she has options.

Teaching generalization helps children modify their responses to various sensory stimuli and social interactions. We want children to use their basic tools for reacting with greater control and thought in lots of different situations, not just in the specific environment of the classroom. In order to do this, children must be able to inhibit or limit out-of-control responses and to plan how to respond instead (Riley et al., 2008).

Being able to attend to sensory data, which includes attending to social behaviors, is the result of increasing skills in perspective taking: understanding what other people think, feel, and know. Learning to attend to what is actually happening instead of automatically communicating, "Get away from me," comes from being exposed to a variety of teaching approaches: modeling, direct instruction, coaching, experiencing consequences (both negative and positive), discussion, practice, and even self-talk (Curtis and Carter, 2003).

As you develop a set of activities to help children modify intense and even repressed reactions, increase skills for intentional and thoughtful action, and build a more positive and authentic self-image, consider three points:

- Children who have experience with stress, trauma, and anxiety are faced with a unique challenge—they are focused on worry and dread about the future. They are often unaware of this perspective, but it limits their capacity to gain needed sensory, verbal, and social information from their immediate experiences. To become more aware and present in the moment, they need assistance from adults who can guide them away from tension and worry.
- For activities that focus on reducing tension, building awareness, and increasing sensory integration to be effective, they must consistently include opportunity for physical

engagement such as resting, moving, observing, and listening; guided adult instruction; and the use of appropriate vocabulary, both verbal and, when necessary, nonverbal.

- Children need practice and repeated exposure to activities and experiences that build the foundation for stress-symptom reduction. Activities should progress throughout the year and include opportunities for children to see adults modeling the behaviors we hope they will adopt.

The three activity categories listed on the following pages focus on different but interrelated types of self-regulation enhancing abilities:

- **Strengthening emotional-physical stability:** When children learn to reduce anxiety and intense reactions by calming their bodies and minds, these skills support the higher-order cognitive ability to detect, identify, and respond to sensory and social cues and information.
- **Expanding awareness and sensory sensitivity:** As children learn to appreciate differences in sensory data through three senses—smell, taste, and touch—they become better able to use more thoughtful methods to sort out and understand the environment and its characteristics.
- **Enhancing the body-brain connection:** Strengthening communication between different areas of the brain, called *cross-lateral functioning,* can expand memory and the capacity for acquiring new skills and can support the use of new skills in novel situations.

Executive thinking skills are the ultimate tools for helping children manage emotions, behaviors, and interactions with others. This higher-order ability, often impaired by the effects of stress and trauma, can be enhanced when children are better able to modify their responses and attend without worry to what is happening in the present. Frequent opportunities to use regulating skills strengthen children's sense of well-being.

BREATHING

One essential skill for children is to intentionally control their breathing. Taking slow, deep breaths can provide a multitude of positive outcomes. Being mindful of this breathing process is key to connecting the physiological benefits with those related to cognitive functioning. Mindful breathing has been shown to reduce blood pressure and the production of stress hormones, but most importantly, it reduces anxiety and worry. Focusing on the process of deep, slow breathing reduces impulsive thought patterns, increases attention to detail, and reduces the constant worrying about what is next and imagining the future (Wickelgren, 2012). The website www.mindfulschools.org offers numerous techniques for mindful breathing. Take the time to learn just a few exercises, and give the children the opportunity to practice every day.

I offer a number of general suggestions for each of the three activity categories. Some of these activities easily can be done with individual children or in a small group setting. I encourage you to use these activities with children who have ongoing concerns with stress. This is certainly not a complete list of suggested activities; I have included additional resources in the appendix on page 151.

Strengthening Emotional-Physical Stability

SKILLS
- Awareness of the rhythm of body movement
- Identification of body movement
- Awareness of body location in physical space
- Awareness of the sensation of breathing and changes in breathing
- Awareness of change in physical sensations related to touch, smell, sound, and light
- Use of calming techniques in anxiety-producing situations

BREATHING AND MINDFULNESS ACTIVITIES
Slow and mindful breathing helps children calm the body and establish a sense of restorative balance. A few tips:
- Do breathing and mindfulness activities three times a week for a minimum of 15 minutes each time.
- Deep breathing to reduce immediate stress, panic, or anxiety requires no fewer than three deep, slow breaths and should continue for two full minutes.
- Darken the room or dim the lights as much as possible.

- Minimize external noise distractions.
- If desired, use a relaxing scent such as lavender, peppermint, or pine. Use essential oils rather than an air freshener—perfumed scents do not have the same sensory quality as oils. Keep the oil out of reach of the children.
- It is helpful for the adult to walk around and between the children, repeating the relaxation and breathing sequence in a calm, quiet voice with occasional touches for children who have difficulty with stillness.
- At times children may also need visual and tangible reminders for remembering relaxation exercises. Using sound, such as a small gong or bell, to begin and end a relaxation session can help them remember. Once they are familiar with the activities, they can hold small stuffed animals or special handkerchiefs and can use picture cards to remind themselves of how to do the exercises.

BASIC STEPS FOR BREATHING AND RELAXATION

1. Ask the children to lie on their backs on mats or large towels. Space them far enough apart so they cannot easily touch each other and each child has a sense of personal space.
2. Ask them to put their hands at their sides or palms down on their stomachs.
3. Tell the children that they are going to slow down their bodies and minds. Ask them to listen with their ears and to rest all the parts of their bodies. Ask them to close their eyes and put their hands on their tummies.
4. Tell them to take a deep breath (pause 2–3 seconds), then breathe out through their mouths with their lips pursed. Ask them to feel their tummies go up as they breathe in and go down as they breathe out. Repeat two or three times.
5. Ask them to breathe in, and then see if they can make their breath go out slowly until you count to the number six. The best way to do this is to blow their breath out through their mouths as if they were slowly blowing up balloons. Let them practice, and count to six as they are breathing out.

6. Ask them to take a breath, feeling their tummies go up, and then let the breath out slowly, feeling their tummies go down. Repeat two or three times.
7. Begin again with slow breathing in and out, tummies going up and down.

Executive thinking skills are the ultimate tools for helping children manage emotions, behaviors, and interactions with others.

PROGRESSIVE RELAXATION

Add progressive relaxation to slow, deep breathing by asking the children to think about images of warm sun or warm water. Ask them to imagine the warmth progressively touching their faces, arms, hands, backs, chests, stomachs, legs, and feet so they relax each part of the body.

VARY THE BASIC BREATHING PROCESS

- Ask the children to slowly blow up an imaginary balloon.
- Place small stuffed animals on their tummies, and ask them to watch the animals slowly rise and then slowly, gently sink down.
- Ask the children to slowly blow on their hands and arms, pretending to push away imaginary clouds, feathers, or snowflakes.
- Breathe while listening for specific sounds on soothing recordings such as water on rocks, birds, or waves (Greenland, 2010).

END THE BREATHING ACTIVITY

After 10 minutes or so, mention that it is time to end relaxation and breathing time. Ask the children to take two more quiet breaths, then to sit up and place their hands on their knees. Ask them to take two more deep breaths, breathing out through their mouths. If their eyes are closed, ask them to open their eyes.

At this point, you may ask questions about how the children's bodies feel now after breathing. Ask them what they heard, what they

remember thinking about, what they felt with their hands, or other reflective questions that focus on the physical sensation of being quiet. Let them know that when they feel scared, worried, or angry, they can take three long, deep breaths. Breathing this way can help them feel stronger and not so worried or mad.

ACTIVITIES FOR FOCUSED, QUIET RELAXATION

- **Sand trays:** Provide a small tray or pan filled with sand for a child to use in a quiet area. The child may wish to explore the sand with her fingers or by playing with small toy animals or people. The smooth, soothing tactile quality of the sand is a calming alternative to more vigorous social activity.

- **Fine motor activities:** Provide lacing cards, marble mazes, matching blocks, or other quiet materials. The child can focus on sorting, order, sequence, and so on. Children who find order, sequencing, and manipulation with their hands to be soothing may be calmed by these activities and may feel a sense of mastery. Some children benefit from holding fidget toys during circle time or when doing some table activities. Bilmes (2011) suggests offering a child who seems a bit frantic and disorganized a small (four-to-eight-piece) puzzle that he can easily complete. The puzzle can become a symbolic way to put things back together. He can sit alone, away from the busy classroom. The teacher can support the child's sense of calm and mastery by saying, "You are putting the pieces back where they belong," or "Now, the pieces fit together, and you got them all in place."
- **Listening to music:** Let a child rest quietly while listening to calming music. Music in a major key with both orchestral and choral elements or with background nature sounds is most soothing. Some children may find certain sounds stressful or irritating, so teachers may want to have them listen to the music beforehand. Music where the tempo is about 60 beats per minute has also been shown to be more relaxing than those with a faster or even slower pace.

- **Taking a break:** Give a child a short break from the classroom activity. Letting her accompany a teacher on a task such as photocopying, taking a few things out to the car, or taking forms to the main office can provide an opportunity for rebalance. These options should involve doing tasks not typically associated with the general routine of the classroom and should not be done as punishment. Discussion of inappropriate behavior is not the goal of this "time away"; these experiences are simply short breaks from the intensity and self-directed control that many children sometimes find overwhelming.

- **Practicing yoga:** Simple stretching and breathing exercises in a quiet setting with calming music can help a child refocus. Tai-chi, in a version appropriate for children in groups of no more than three, can also be a relaxing break.

- **Quiet time:** Children can benefit from sitting and looking at books of serene places, peaceful animals, colors, and so on while holding a large stuffed "quiet bear" or doll or while listening to quiet music. Some may wish to spend time in a rocking or swinging chair. Others may wish to walk slowly and silently (outdoors or indoors), slowly blow bubbles, or lie for a short while with a lightly weighted bag (scented, perhaps) on their eyes, chests, or bodies.

We can help children modify their reactions to stress and undo some old patterns by providing multiple options for calming the body, increasing familiarity with

nonthreatening sensory experiences, and providing alternatives for the brain to process these types of experiences.

REBALANCING VOCABULARY

balance	rise (up)	neck	feet
quiet	fall (down)	shoulders	notice
relax	still	chest	listen
rest	calm	stomach	feel
blow	peaceful	back	think about
slowly	breathe	legs	
gently	head	knees	

Expanding Awareness and Sensory Sensitivity

SKILLS

- Awareness of sensory cues
- Identification and use of description, such as *loud, soft,* and "like the outdoors"
- Familiarity with sensory experiences
- Listening
- Observation
- Appreciation
- Desensitization to overstimulating or unpleasant experiences

For activities where children might easily see what they are smelling, tasting, or touching, try using a container such as a shoe box so children will not be able to see the contents and guess rather than using their appropriate sense.

Children will remember their preferences better if they are documented. Create simple books, such as *What I Like and Don't Like,* or graph the children's preferences.

SENSORY DISCRIMINATION ACTIVITIES: TASTE AND SMELL

These activities help children identify and compare the varying qualities of sensory information. Children learn to concentrate on one or two characteristics of sensory data, which will expand their repertoire or catalogue of sensory experiences. The more discriminating experiences children have, the greater their capacity to see differences and similarities and to make comparisons. For children who have sensory-related stress triggers (especially smell, touch, or taste), identifying sensory information, understanding personal preferences, labeling, and comparison may offer ways to diminish the intensity of these experiences (Eliason and Jenkins, 1994).

- Similar items do not always smell or taste the same. Try offering different types of flowers for the child to smell, such as roses, honeysuckle, and lavender. Offer different types of cereal or varieties of apples for the child to taste. Talk about how the items are similar and how they differ.
- Some foods look very similar but do not taste the same. Compare the tastes of salt and sugar or cornstarch and flour.
- Some items may have the same smell but may be very different. Discuss how lemon-scented soap and a real lemon are similar and different.
- Smells and tastes of foods may change through cooking or drying. Sample raw and cooked carrots or grapes and raisins. Compare bread dough and fresh-baked bread. How do the foods change?

SENSORY DISCRIMINATION ACTIVITIES: TOUCH

Describing the sense of touch can be confusing for children. We touch something and call that process *feeling.* We use the sense of touch to discern the texture of an object. We do not use the sense of touch to sense an emotion. In the activities in this section, be as specific as possible when describing texture. For example, it is more accurate to say, "The fur on the bunny is soft when you touch it," than it is to say, "The bunny is soft," or "The bunny feels soft," (Eliason and Jenkins, 1994).

- Compare different textures on the same object: Single items can vary in texture. Encourage children to compare the textures of the skin on their feet with the skin on their faces. Compare the different textures of a tree: leaves, bark, branches. Teach the children words to describe these textures.

- Different items can have the same texture: Compare a plastic block with a glass. Compare a brick and cement. Explore a cotton ball and a piece of velvet fabric. If the children close their eyes, can they discern a difference?

- Texture can change through heat, cold, drying, sanding, cooking, or changes from nature such as erosion: Compare a piece of quartz and sand, water and ice, a rough piece of wood and a sanded piece of wood, plums and prunes, or a whole potato and mashed potatoes. How have the textures changed?

- We can have a feeling about something we touch; for example, I may like the feeling of soft, smooth velvet, but I may dislike the feeling of a slippery worm. Encourage the children to use vocabulary to compare what items feel like when they touch them: *smooth, bumpy, gritty, cold, gooey, sticky, hard, fuzzy, wet, sharp.* Compare these words to emotional feelings the children may have about the items and their textures.

Enhancing Body-Brain Integration

SKILLS

- Use of auditory cues
- Use of visual cues
- Use of kinesthetic cues
- Following directions
- Adhering to rules despite contradictory information
- Balance
- Coordination of body movement in space
- Expanding inhibition skills
- Vocabulary

Try Run-Stop-Run to teach following directions and cross-lateral brain function.

1. Have the children run 10–20 steps and then stop.
2. Tell them to put their arms over their heads and then say, "One, two, three!"
3. Run again for 10–20 steps.

Any variation of running, stopping with some upper-body movement, and verbalization will work.

BUILDING CONFIDENCE

1. Ask the children to stand as tall and as big as they possibly can without moving about.
2. Tell them to breathe very deeply and let the air out slowly.
3. Ask them to pretend there is a string attached to the top of their heads and it is pulling up so they are tall. Tell them their shoulders should be down away from the ears and back, feet slightly apart, and arms down at their sides.
4. If possible, ask the children to stand "big" for about 30–45 seconds. If this activity is repeated frequently, children can be asked to remember what they feel like when they are standing "big."

BODY-BRAIN INTEGRATION ACTIVITIES

- Run, stop, change direction games:
    - red light-green light
    - freeze tag
    - duck-duck-goose
    - Simon says
    - ready, set, go
    - jumping in place
- Taking turns, changing direction, and memory games:
    - I Spy
    - memory board games
    - easy board games such as Hi-Ho Cherry-O or Candy Land
    - B-I-N-G-O
- Coordinating physical movement with auditory cues and/or visual cues:
    - moving to music with varied tempos
    - singing or movement activities
    - using visual cues, such as a picture of a bee for moving very fast and a picture of an elephant for moving very slowly
    - "ice skating" on a bare floor (using socks for skates)
    - throwing at a target
    - playing catch
    - t-ball
- Cross-lateral movements and balance activities:
    - marching
    - marching with sticks, ribbons, or musical instruments
    - swinging arms in different directions

- crawling over an obstacle course
- practicing moving one arm, then the other, across the midline of the body
- walking backward, sideways, with eyes closed
- walking with arms overhead or touching the shoulders
- touching opposite arm to knee or opposite arm to shoulder
- touching opposite hand to toe
- crab walking
- using balance beams or floor tape for walking variations, such as tip-toe, backward, fast and slow
- hopping and walking with objects in hands or on the head, such as ribbons, sticks, or bells
- hopscotch
- jump rope
- parachute games
- floor hockey
- simple relay games
- full-body stretching, such as being a crab (curled up), then becoming a giant starfish
- Vocabulary:
  - Positional/directional words: *under, over, on top of, around, through, below, under*
  - Action words: *walk, jump, hop, run, skip, leap, gallop, slide, climb, throw, catch, kick, hit, bend, twist, push, pull, swing, sit, stand, roll, freeze, step, jump, squeeze, hold (tight, loose), start, stop, begin, quit, open, close, shut, hurry*
  - Temporal words (awareness of speed, timing, duration, and rhythm): *high, low, middle, smooth, jerky, bent, twisted, fast, slow, long, short, heavy, light*

Incorporating Activities in the Classroom

Include self-regulation activities in your classroom curriculum on a daily basis; they will not be effective if they are used sporadically or for a short period of time. Incorporate the activities as part of a planned theme, such as My Five Senses, or as part of the regular classroom routine. Work with the children to explore sensory discrimination activities throughout the year, moving from basic identification to more complex comparison and discrimination experiences. The skills developed through sensory awareness are progressive and sequential and require experience over time. Repeating activities several weeks apart can also provide awareness of changes in preferences, in skills of detection, and refinement of sensory awareness. Relaxation activities are an everyday "must" (if possible) and will be most effective if repeated with slight variations over the school year.

Helping children increase self-regulation skills goes far beyond implementing the activities and concepts listed in this chapter. It also involves having a guidance plan in place that supports the development of strong, supportive, prosocial skills for all children. Helping children gain skills for conflict resolution, negotiation, collaboration, and acting with kindness and compassion is essential for ensuring and strengthening positive experiences for all children, not just those with stress-related concerns.

Increasing children's capacity for monitoring and managing their physical and emotional responses to sensory stimuli is an important project for classroom teachers to undertake. When children have greater skills in identifying those sensations, events, and memories that induce stress reactions, they will be better able to decrease the negative effects of stress on their own. Reducing the intensity and perceived disorganization of negative sensory stimuli can increase a child's cognitive capacity, especially in the areas of executive function. Children who are better able to authentically engage with their physical environment and other people will be better able to navigate and adjust to the demands of their worlds. Skills that foster adaptability and flexibility are essential tools for making childhood an easier and richer experience.

Ideas for Practice

The information in this chapter focuses on building children's physical and sensory self-regulation skills with the ultimate goal of increasing a capacity for social and intellectual adaptation and flexibility. Many of the activities that support this goal are concrete, focused, and intentional—not very "artsy" or creative. So perhaps a bit of inventive conversation will help children use their imaginations. The following list of questions is intended for use with small groups of children. The goal is not to solicit deep thought, intellectually challenging or even socially important conversation, but to give children something a bit different to consider. Encountering the creative and innovative ideas of others is one way to build connections with other children and get to know new things from them as people.

Encountering the creative and innovative ideas of others is one way to build connections with other children and get to know new things from them as people.

1. If you were a superhero, what one power would you have? How would it work? Why did you want to have that power? What do you think you might look like as that superhero? What would your superhero name be?

2. Pretend that you have a pair of magic wings in your closet that will take you anywhere you want to go. Where would you like to fly? What do you think you would see?

3. If you could spend one day as an animal, which one would you choose to be? What do you think you would do? What do you think your day might be like? What would you eat? What other animals do you think you would see?

4. How do you think peanut butter is made? Why do you think the sky is blue? How do you think shows get onto the TV? How did

the elephant's nose (giraffe's neck, flamingo's legs, monkey's tail) get so long? How does the chicken get inside chicken nuggets?

5. Ask the children to complete some common proverbs. Accept any answer the children give.
   a. Better to be safe than _____
   b. Never underestimate the power of _____
   c. Where there's smoke there's _____
   d. Better late than _____
   e. Strike when the _____
   f. Happy is the bride who(m) _____
   g. A penny saved is _____
   h. Children should be seen and not _____
   (**Note:** If you are unfamiliar with these proverbs, the missing words are as follows: a. sorry; b. a woman; c. fire; d. never; e. iron is hot; f. the sun shines on; g. a penny earned; h. heard.)

6. What does the president of the United States do?

7. Would you rather live in the ocean or on the moon? in the sky or under the ground? on top of a tall mountain or in a tree house? at the zoo or on an airplane? What would be the best thing about living there?

8. Would you rather be a giant ant or a tiny elephant? have a really big nose or a tiny nose in your ear that no one could see? be very, very tall so you could see over all the people or very, very small so you could be anywhere? jump into a pool of marshmallows or a pool of Jell-O? have stretchy arms or wheels on the bottoms of your feet? be a pencil or a rubber band? be invisible or be able to fly?

9. What would be the best thing about being a dog? cat? dragon? bird? Why? What would be the worst thing about being that creature?

10. Ask the children to complete these story starters:
    ■ Once upon a time I was walking along and saw a _____.
    ■ I was really surprised (or scared) when I looked into my lunchbox and found a _____.
    ■ One day when I came into my classroom at _____ (fill in school name), I saw a big, green, hairy, stinky _____ sitting on the floor (hanging from the ceiling; eating a snack).

Building Self-Competence

FIVE THINGS WE KNOW

❶ Through strong connection to their classroom community and learning to better manage self-regulation, children can develop resilience to stress.

❷ In classroom settings, everyday experiences that calm the body, expand awareness of sensory sensitivity, and enhance body-brain integration are ways to support self-regulation.

❸ Developing greater expertise in self-regulation can positively influence a child's learning, relationships, and experience strengths.

❹ Strengthening children's self-regulation skills can provide opportunity to "mend" sensory-physical, as well as social-emotional, experience filters and provide for the possibility of more authentic experiences and learning.

❺ One important goal in working with children affected by stress and trauma is to build skills in a variety of areas as a means to support children across the domains of development: emotional-social, physical, and cognitive.

What Is Self-Competence?

A self-competent person is skilled, capable, experienced, able to meet her basic needs without being highly dependent on others, able to do a variety of things well, reasonably confident (but not arrogant), and socially pleasant. Self-competence is the awareness of interrelated perceptions of one's own abilities, self-efficacy, and value as a person (Hyson, 2004; Riley et al., 2008). The awareness of one's talents, skills, and capacity for getting things accomplished can help build the most important attribute of self-competence: self-worth.

Having a healthy sense of self-competence would seem to be a very good thing! This sense of competence develops over time, beginning in early childhood and in relationship to interactions with other people. For children to have a sense of their competence, they must clearly know what skills and abilities they have and of what value these qualities are to themselves and other people.

Stress, Trauma, and Self-Competence

Aside from the well-documented damaging effects of stress and trauma on physical health, for many children their self-esteem is also negatively affected. The lives of stress-affected children are dominated by trying to meet their basic needs for survival while coping with the impact of adversity. Much of their "negative me" awareness develops as children mature and become aware of the skills other children may have that they do not.

Many children with significant stress histories have missed opportunities to appropriately experience how social environments work. They have little knowledge about how to work with others, lend a hand, and thoughtfully engage with their learning experiences. Each child's missed opportunities are highly individualistic, so some children may have strong abilities in some areas but may be lacking in others.

Amy

Amy is almost six years old. She knows the basics of how to read and gets along well with others, but she has poor self-care skills. She is unable to easily put on her clothes, rarely washes her hands and face, and has poor table manners that cause other children to ridicule and avoid her at meals.

Martin

Martin is highly self-sufficient in getting his basic needs met, especially his self-care responsibilities. He packs his lunch by himself and gets ready in the morning for kindergarten. However, he lacks awareness of and skills for how he might contribute to and belong among his classmates. He rarely picks up after himself without being told, seems unaware of the feelings and behaviors of others, and he gives few details when asked to complete the "Everything I Know about Me" exercise, even at the end of his kindergarten year.

For children who have such profiles, strengthening self-competence by building on their existing strengths and skills is important. Developing and increasing types of skills that children can attribute to themselves can positively shape and strengthen their resilience (Breslin, 2005; Bruce and Cairone, 2011).

Experiences to Build

Self-Competence

With positive support from other people, children construct their own meaning of competence and worth primarily through experiences that result in visible accomplishments, such as writing numbers, riding a bicycle with training wheels, or painting a picture with story content. Children acquire competence when they have active involvement over time with experiences that lead to an increase in knowledge or skills (Katz and McClellan, 1991; Landy, 2002). For children to build a healthy sense of competence and worth, they need opportunities to constructively participate in society:

- **The culture of childhood:** Children need to experience how to interact, communicate, and be included in essential creative play.
- **The parallel culture of adulthood:** Children learn through the appropriate experiences provided by family and community. (They do not need to have adult experiences firsthand!)
- **The practices and rituals of society:** Children learn through the social, ethnic, linguistic, and spiritual cultures that define their evolving personal and family identities.

For many children these big-picture interactions occur with relative ease as they become socialized, more mature, and capable of being included in more experiences out in the world. For children who have significant stress and trauma histories, their encounters with many of these different cultures have produced negative outcomes. They need additional support, even intervention, in order to fill in the missing pieces and to understand themselves as significant people.

Self-competence skills include learning to complete tasks, engage in social interaction with other children in positive ways, move the body with coordination and agility, regulate strong emotions, have a strong sense of self, and display interest and curiosity (Marion, 2011; Bredekamp and Copple, 2009). For stress-impacted children, research has identified areas of vulnerability in developing self-competence:

- awareness and observation (visual and auditory) skills,
- developing and using a personal problem-solving system, and
- participating in meaningful work.

By helping children develop in these areas, teachers and caregivers can help them construct a catalogue of personal competencies, an inventory of accomplishments. When children possess an awareness and evidence of their own skills and talents, they can build an authentic and positive sense of self. Knowing that she can observe and analyze the world with skill, can better understand what people are expressing with their emotions, and can make a real contribution will go a long way in erasing some of the damaging effects of stress and trauma in a child.

MASTERY

Mastery involves having knowledge, ability, and accomplishment. Having mastered a task or understood a concept, we can move on to other more challenging or interesting goals. Accomplishing meaningful tasks is an essential feature of childhood and an important milestone for all children. What results is a strengthened intrinsic drive for learning and connection (Gartrell, 2012). Mastery helps move children from being dependent on adult acknowledgement of their "goodness" by providing concrete evidence of their own value and achievement. Success is not defined through rating these accomplishments; perfect is not part of the model of mastery for children. Instead, initiative and completion are most important. The phrase "good enough is good enough" is what accomplishment and self-worth should entail when one is four, five, or six years old.

Three Strategies for Building a Portfolio of Competence

Expanding awareness and observation skills, developing and using a personal problem-solving system, and participating in meaningful work can increase competence, especially for stress-affected children. If children can increase their skills and abilities, their competency will have a ripple effect on other areas of development.

Expanding Awareness and Observation Skills

Helping children increase their observation skills centers on increasing their ability to more accurately see and hear what is happening in their physical environments. Children's observation skills are limited by inexperience, immaturity, and often their patterns of sensory response to stress. Becoming more aware and attuned to what one sees and hears is an important skill for children to build. This is especially true when they may have already acquired somewhat faulty observation strategies and find the physical environment overwhelming or threatening. When a child is able to more accurately read his physical-social environment, he is more likely to find meaning, create opportunity for making connections with others, and find interesting things to investigate.

Becoming more fluent in the skills of observation includes learning to pay attention to and identify visual and auditory cues and details, identifying and using verbal or symbolic language to describe what has been seen or heard, and, when necessary, drawing more objective conclusions. The ability to interpret and comprehend, for example, other people's facial and body language requires focused observation and is one of the core capabilities for building emotional competence skills (Bilmes, 2011; Landy, 2002).

Learning to focus on details as well as the big picture takes maturity and practice. For many young children, their visual

Helping Them Heal

lives are filled with action: scanning for the activity while simultaneously noticing interesting details of everything from bugs on the ground to who just came in the door. Visual focus rapidly changes as new sensory data such as sounds, smells, and movement draws attention to something more interesting or concerning. Children who are anxious and affected negatively by stress experiences may focus their visual and auditory awareness on sensations that indicate—realistically or not—that risk and threat may be present. Fear and threat limit children's capacity to view the world as a neutral place or at least as not a full-time threat (Summers and Chazen-Cohen, 2012). Children can learn to thoughtfully observe, with sufficient time and guided instruction. Having more refined skills in reading the environment provides children with more accurate information and the possibility of participating in their world with greater engagement and, maybe, less worry.

Children's observation skills are limited by inexperience, immaturity, and often their patterns of sensory response to stress.

WHAT DO I SEE? VISUAL OBSERVATION STUDY

Steps to Strengthen Visual Observation Skills

1. Visually scan the environment.
2. Identify what is in the environment.
3. Verbally articulate what is seen.
4. Recall the images.

How to Do It

1. Place children in small groups of three or four.
2. Offer pictures, especially artwork, drawings, illustrations, and photographs, for the children to look at. The pictures should be at least 24" x 24" images of one or two people doing a simple, everyday activity, such as eating lunch, picking flowers, or walking down the street. If there is not already one given by the artist, be sure to give a name to each picture that is used for observation study.
3. Ask the children a series of questions that draw specific attention to the "story" and details of the picture. Modify the questions for the level of understanding of the specific group of children.
   - Are there people or animals in the picture? If so, how many?
   - What event is happening?

- Is the picture showing the indoors or the outdoors?
- What details do you see (hair color, dress, age, gender, activity, and so forth)?
- What objects are in the picture?
- What time of day, place, season, and weather do you see?
- What colors, shapes, kinds of lines are used in the picture?
- What might the person in the picture be thinking about?
- What do you think the artist wanted to tell us about this person or event?

4. Put the picture down, and ask the children to tell you what they remember about it. Ask what they would tell someone else about this picture, what they liked about the picture, and what they disliked.

5. Repeat this activity over time with increasingly complex images. Practiced observation and recall might eventually include up to four pictures being shown during a 15-minute observation practice session.

As children become more skilled at identifying characteristics and talking about what they see, introduce more complex images, such as drawings, posters, and art prints with more action, features to discuss, and more potential for creative interpretation by the children. With practice, the children will need to spend less time on slow, careful observation; their attention will become more focused.

If needed, use short DVD or video content selections as a bridge for learning to observe in real life. These selections can be replayed to check for the accuracy and creativity of the children's responses. Also, it may be helpful to mute the sound to focus the children's attention on the visual stimuli.

Once children have become more proficient at identifying characteristics of static images and recorded action, they can bring their observation skills to use with real-life situations. Having children observe simple social interactions within their classroom or on a field trip where there are two or three people involved in an activity requires a high level of skill. Prior experience and strong teacher support can make these kinds of real-life observations interesting and skill building.

With adult guidance, the practice of observing very short three- to five-minute play sessions, transition times, and teacher activity can be used. Children can learn to objectively observe, "take notes," and make a report on any number of situations: nature study, people watching, activity outside the classroom such as trucks unloading supplies or the number and kinds of cars going by the center are all possibilities.

Observation study may be more interesting if children have special tools to use, such as old eyeglass frames with no lenses or paper tubes taped together like binoculars. Play a game such as I Spy. Practice observation study weekly and keep a record of what the children observe. This last step is particularly important for documenting changes in skills and recording the children's accomplishments. Note that some children have little interest in visual stimuli and, despite sincere commitment and skill on the part of a teacher, will not find observation experiences interesting because of their dominant learning style.

Being able to attend to sound is part of developing more accurate and mature observation skills as well. Many of the experiences that foster visual observation can be used to increase children's abilities to listen more carefully and identify sounds and information they receive from this sensory source. Learning to listen is essential for children's success as they mature and are expected to use auditory processes for a significant part of their academic learning (Kostelnik et al., 2011).

Listening skills include being able to differentiate qualities of sound, such as pitch, source, intention, volume, and rhythm, as well as identifying and describing what has been heard. Asking children to focus their attention on sounds should begin with identification of familiar sounds and then progress to unfamiliar sounds (Eliason and Jenkins, 1994). Although most children have extensive experience in listening to adult and child conversations, being read to, and listening to music, and so on, many may need additional guidance in order to listen with greater accuracy.

One of the major expectations for children in elementary school is the capacity to comprehend spoken text and respond appropriately (Bredekamp and Copple, 2009). Auditory memory can be improved when children have the opportunity to center their attention on key features of auditory awareness (Gillanders and Castro, 2011; Jalongo, 2008). Classroom teachers can easily implement experiences that support children's awareness of sounds when they build activities around a set of concepts. Observation of sounds requires careful attention to the qualities of what is heard and then connecting the sensory experience with descriptive words. Building a strong understanding of the relationship between sound and what it is or what it means is best developed through the use of concepts.

Teachers can foster children's listening skills through practices very similar to those outlined for visual observation. Children may need additional preparation using focused lessons, as their listening skills are so closely linked to visual cues; listening takes special effort. It is also important that teachers prepare children for experiences with sound and that children listen with their eyes closed when they can to help focus awareness on sound.

WHAT DO I HEAR? AUDITORY OBSERVATION STUDY
Steps to Strengthen Auditory Observation Skills
  1. Explore different categories of sounds:
     - musical
     - machines
     - animal
     - nature

- at home
- people

2. Explore different characteristics of sounds or ways sounds make us feel:
   - heavy
   - light
   - noisy
   - frightening
   - exciting
   - gross
   - soft
   - happy

3. Explore the uses of sounds and the information sounds give us:
   - bells used to tell us time of day
   - doorbell
   - phone ringing
   - baby crying
   - horn honking
   - announcements on public address systems
   - warnings from sirens
   - different kinds of machines and what they do
   - locations of the sources of sounds

4. Sounds may be so quiet we cannot hear them:
   - snow
   - worms crawling
   - bugs flying
   - lights coming on

5. Some things we can hear but may not see:
   - wind
   - stomach growling
   - air conditioning coming on

6. Sounds that we hear when people talk can tell us what they might be feeling or doing:
   - loud can be angry, directive, or happy
   - quiet can be sad, a secret, or a whisper
   - yelling at a sporting event
   - singing in the shower
   - telling a story

Observation of sounds requires careful attention to the qualities of what is heard and then connecting the sensory experience with descriptive words.

7. People use sounds to tell us things we need to know. When we listen we can hear what their voices are telling us:
   - instructions
   - warnings
   - information
   - funny stories
   - emotions

(Concepts 1–4 were adapted from Eliason and Jenkins, 1994.)

A SPECIAL TYPE OF OBSERVATION: WHAT ARE PEOPLE FEELING?

One of the most significant skills children are expected to acquire is that of understanding the emotional expression of others. Being able to determine if someone is sad, happy, angry, frustrated, worried, confused, or curious requires awareness of nonverbal facial and body-language cues. It requires that children are able to associate a name with those cues and associate the name with the matching behaviors and feelings. Learning the appropriate names and making the connection to physical cues takes experience, guidance, and skill in observation.

Caregivers and teachers can help children with this complex task by giving them opportunities to associate feeling names with physical characteristics that typify the emotion. Focusing a child's awareness on the specific features of the human face that are the primary areas where emotional change takes place—eyes, mouth, facial movement—is the key to helping children differentiate these subtle but telling changes.

Steps to Strengthen Feeling Recognition Skills
1. Use photographs rather than drawings to give children more opportunities to refine their understanding of emotional states and their associated terms and meanings. Use picture cards of the same face in various emotional states, such as sad, angry, confused, and happy. When children are first learning to match emotions with their descriptive labels, viewing different faces depicting different emotions may be more difficult because there is more sensory data to sort through.
2. Once children are able to easily identify and label different emotions on the same face, add additional images of these

same emotional expressions on faces that vary by gender, age, ethnicity, and dress. Make picture cards, both drawings and photographs, of people in different emotional states to help children expand their skills.

3. Add full-body images, not just faces, to provide more sensory data and require more refined observation.

4. Being able to discern feelings expressed in real life is the final step. Children can use the guided observation skills to observe children in their own classroom, adults in their immediate environment, and, finally, people outside their familiar world. Help children recognize, label, and then discuss what they are observing and what these feelings mean.

The ultimate goal of helping children expand their emotional awareness and emotional expression is to teach them how to identify their own emotional states and express what they are feeling (Bilmes, 2011; Epstein, 2011).

Developing and Using a Personal Problem-Solving System

One of the most appropriate methods for helping children manage the emotionally and sometimes physically challenging aspects of their lives is the use of conflict resolution strategies. Multiple variations exist, but the practice is widely taught from preschool through high school. These strategies focus primarily on helping children resolve arguments and disagreements defined by tension, confusion, and heightened emotional intensity (Wheeler, 2004). Research findings on their long-term use has provided solid evidence of their effectiveness in moderating children's negative feelings and in decreasing aggression and conflict levels in classrooms (Bredekamp, 2010; Wheeler, 2004).

For children, especially those affected by the disruptive effects of stress and trauma, the ability to think in a sequential, ordered, and disciplined way is often impossible (Summers and Chazan-Cohen, 2012; Steele and Malchiodi, 2012). It may be easier for these children to make a quick choice, judge something on how it feels rather than how it exists in reality, postpone making any determination, or avoid ever coming to a conclusion. All of these possible approaches are common strategies used by all children but are more frequently seen in those affected by stress.

Help children create their own problem-solving strategy to use as a tool for making all kinds of decisions. Such decisions can include managing minor conflicts, selecting what paper color to use or which game to play, identifying what feelings they have, or finding someone who can help with a problem. Being able to own the process of making decisions is empowering and essential as children grow and move away from family and the more relationship-based early childhood support systems.

Most problem-solving systems have similar steps in common:
- identification of the problem or situation,
- generation of possible solutions,
- agreement on one selected possibility, and
- implementation.

(Bilmes, 2011; Gartrell, 2012; Wheeler, 2004).

When strong feelings are involved, there may be the additional step of helping children identify their feelings as a way to strengthen thinking skills (Epstein, 2011). These strategies are intended to move children's response patterns from one of confusion and emotionality to a process based on thinking. With these skills, children are better able to generate multiple solutions and to come up with an alternate plan. Kersey and Masterson (2013) note that a child's capacity to come up with more than one solution to a problem is a key factor in resilience.

Steps to Increase Children's Problem-Solving Skills
1. Help the child identify that there is a decision that needs resolution. Making a decision or choice is a cognitive action. The child must learn to identify the issue and state the issue in clear terms using a consistent action phrase: "I have a choice to make, and a choice is something I can think about." The teacher or caregiver can assist the child in identifying who is involved in the choice:
   - **Just the child ("just me"):** Jena has a hard time choosing a snack when there are two or more options. Helping her

decide might involve teaching her to say, "I have a choice to make. This is a choice just for me."

- **Another person with conflict ("myself and _____ , and we each want (to)_____"):** Marcus and Tyler are arguing over who gets to play with the blocks. Helping Marcus resolve the situation might involve having him say, "I have a decision to make. This is a decision with Tyler and me, and we each want to play with the blocks."

2. Help the child generate possible solutions, mentally or verbally. Use words that focus on thinking to avoid confusion, trying to make a choice to please others, and letting feelings dominate the decision:

- Jena can state her choices: "I can choose cheese and crackers or a banana or applesauce. This is a choice just for me. I can do it by myself."
- Marcus can state his possible solutions: "I can walk away and let Tyler play with the blocks. I can push him down and take the blocks. I can ask Teacher Amy to help me with this choice. I have to include Tyler in the choice because there are two of us with a problem."

3. Help the child decide on a first choice and understand that a decision was made:

- Jena can say, "I can choose by myself, and even if I don't like it, it will be okay," or "I thought about which one I like best, and now I can choose a banana," or "This is the snack I choose."
- Marcus will have to negotiate with Tyler at this point. If each child can generate two or three solutions, the expectation is that one will be acceptable to both. Using traditional conflict resolution practices can provide guidance on how to manage the negotiation process (see Epstein, 2011; Gartrell, 2012; Kostelnik et al., 2011). The intent is to have the child verbalize that he has come to a decision: "I have made a decision with Tyler, and we are going to take turns."

TRADITIONAL CONFLICT RESOLUTION PRACTICES

Helping children manage conflict focuses on building their skills so that they can learn to resolve disagreements on their own. Achieving conflict resolution skills requires direction from adults as well as practice.

Step One: The adult quietly intervenes and stops any aggressive behavior, which may also involve taking possession of any item or territory that is in dispute.

Step Two: The adult solicits unedited information from each child about what has happened.

Step Three: The adult summarizes what each child has said and what she understands has happened.

Step Four: The adult asks each child to propose one or two ideas for resolving the disagreement (the adult can suggest additional possibilities if needed).

Step Five: The adult helps the children come to a mutual agreement on a clear, fair resolution.

Step Six: The adult monitors the children to make sure they each adhere to their solution and to insure no further conflict over this particular issue continues.

Step Seven: The adult recognizes the children's effort in resolving their conflict and carrying out their solution and offers concrete, sincere validation.

The key is for the child to specifically articulate that he has made a decision and has said so aloud. Building self-awareness of accomplishment for young children requires that they have concrete evidence, such as in writing, via verbalization, or the fact that an adult notices that an action was taken. Stating that he has made a decision brings identity and closure to the process.

It is in step three where a child develops awareness because the child has demonstrated thinking skills in making a choice. The outcome is actually less important than the process of using a cognitively focused strategy and that the effort was accomplished. Receiving feedback and encouragement from adults—and occasionally another peer—recognizes the achievement and can

Helping Them Heal

help clarify the child's personal confidence and knowledge of his abilities.

Following steps helps children move to more thoughtful processes of decision making. Being able to do so in a variety of circumstances is empowering and provides additional skills of self-control, self-awareness, and independence. Teachers and caregivers can use any variation on the steps presented here or from other resources that appears useful to children. It is not so much the use of one particular strategy but the use of one that is functional for the child. Some children respond to giving their strategy a name, such as "I Can Choose," "Pick 1–2–3," or "I Decide for Me." Helping children feel secure about decision making is the goal, and having a process that removes some of the emotional intensity and insecurity can be of great value.

Participating in Meaningful Work

Children become more aware of their self-worth and value beginning around age four or five (Marion, 2011). This process involves a complex set of cognitive abilities directly influenced by a child's concrete experiences and the child's evaluation of her effectiveness in accomplishing things. Self-evaluation is based on verbal and nonverbal feedback from other people and from the child herself. The child evaluates how capable she assumes herself to be in taking responsibility for self-care, working constructively with others, and completing physical tasks.

Self-esteem is the judging part of self-concept and emerges as children become capable of understanding there are expectations and socially acceptable ways of doing things or looking or behaving (Epstein, 2011; Hendrick, 2003). Young children's criteria for evaluating are very concrete. It is about the outcome, such as completing a school assignment, picking the "right" book for circle time, and getting to the sandbox first to be sure to get the big tractor, rather than the intention or reality: "I tried hard"; "I am fine the way I am"; and "It is okay if I am not first."

When children participate in meaningful work, they gain concrete evidence of their ability to influence their world. Meaningful work involves activities, tasks, and responsibilities that are above and beyond the everyday personal chores necessary for classroom life. Meaningful work is about making a contribution to the classroom that focuses on the community and living with and caring for other people.

MANNERS AND BEING POLITE

Having good manners means being polite, demonstrating respect, and having consideration for others. Helping children learn a basic set of manners and etiquette can be an important way to strengthen their social skills and self-competence. While expectations for manners and etiquette in social settings vary widely by culture, there are some foundational expectations that can be useful for all children. Children's ability to self-regulate and understand behavioral expectations is significantly influenced by developmental differences. For young children, there are two areas where demonstrating socially appropriate behavior is useful: when interacting with others and when eating.

Young children can learn to appropriately use *please, thank you,* and *excuse me.* They can understand that pushing, shoving, throwing objects, yelling, running over other people, and loud talking are often inappropriate behaviors. Help children gain confidence and build skills by practicing socially acceptable behaviors before they go "out in the world."

Managing the physical process of eating and knowing what is expected during meals are big skills for children to accomplish. With practice, guidance, and appropriate expectations, children can make eating experiences more pleasant for themselves and others. Basic etiquette for young children can include properly using a napkin and eating implements, keeping utensils on the table when not in use, chewing slowly, not talking while chewing, keeping food on the plate, asking to have food passed, talking quietly, limiting loud eating noises, and helping to clear the table when the meal is over.

Meaningful work provides opportunities for children to build the skills necessary to actively participate in the tasks of daily living and increases their capacity for independence, initiative, and self-sufficiency. Having responsibility means that you are trusted to undertake and complete a task. Expecting children to be capable of helping out, able to make things better, and able to contribute to the community in which they live is not only developmentally appropriate and empowering, but it signals that children and their efforts are welcome and necessary (Hendrick 1967; Readdick and Douglas, 2000). Experiences with meaningful work—and calling it *work*—provide children with enjoyment of both the process and product of an activity. When things do not go quite as expected— the dustpan tips, the juice spills, the plants are overwatered— children can, with reassurance from adults, learn ways to fix or repair problems or mistakes. Engaging in meaningful work with minimal negative outcomes can be a constructive and natural part of learning (Hendrick, 1967).

When thoughtful adults provide positive models about what work is, they can offer alternatives to more negative and narrow ideas many children possess, such as the idea that work is something grown-ups do for a paycheck, that it is boring, or that it is completely out of reach of a child's efforts and abilities. Adults can explain that, as teachers, their work is to help children learn about the world; learn how to make friends and play together; and begin to learn about science, math, reading, and writing. Children can learn that school is a place where everyone has a job—teachers, bus drivers, office staff, and children! Taking care of the classroom, each other, and the playground is everyone's job, and children have many abilities and ways to help out.

How teachers approach classroom chores by including children in the general upkeep and maintenance of the classroom, its living things, and caring for one another is an important contributor to classroom culture (Readdick and Douglas, 2000). Having responsibilities and identifying these tasks as meaningful work can go a long way to improving children's evolving concepts. Identifying work as something positive, where children can assign meaning beyond how adults define such experiences, is an important understanding for children to construct on their own.

Meaningful work is always context and program specific. When children have the opportunity to do meaningful work within their own classroom, it can be a starting point for developing skills that can be used in the outside world. Through cleaning tables, putting the caps back on markers, picking up trash, or sorting items for recycling, children know they are being asked to care for their own space. With acknowledgement and identification of such efforts, they can more easily identify their impact.

Classroom responsibilities and meaningful work should, of course, be appropriate to the developmental level and abilities of the children. Young four-year-olds will have difficulty emptying a trash can if it is too large; and without supervision and preparation, even a capable six-year-old can drown plants or overfeed the fish. Children need appropriate time for work, real tools and materials for specific tasks, and assignments that are reasonably short or can be broken down into shorter portions (Hendrick, 1967).

Asking children to help out with tasks outside the classroom extends the experience and is especially useful for children who are kindergarten age or older. Walking the outside of the building (if appropriate) to check for litter, taking attendance in another room, helping younger children put on coats, helping the secretary with recycling, and cleaning tables in the lunch room are all options for making a difference for other people.

SAFETY

Child safety is always the first priority when deciding on tasks children can undertake, regardless of child interest or skill. Activities that children might be capable of may pose a health hazard or may not be allowed in some locations. Examples include cleaning animal or bird cages, cleaning aquariums, picking up trash outside, some aspects of food preparation, and use of small appliances and machines. Allowing children to run short errands within a confined school building has to be considered from all possible safety angles. Children should never be responsible for deciding if something they are asked to do is safe; nor should they be placed at risk because adult supervision is lacking. **All work activities for children must be closely supervised by adults.**

The following list identifies just some options for children's meaningful work in classroom settings:

- helping with snack or lunch service and cleanup
- washing and drying dishes after snack or a meal
- watering classroom plants
- planting, weeding, watering, and harvesting in a garden
- cleaning tables, shelves, play structures, art materials and supplies, or toys
- taking messages from one location to another
- taking down bulletin-board displays
- hosing off sidewalks or sweeping outside areas
- oiling tricycles when squeaky
- washing outdoor toys and equipment
- sweeping and mopping indoor floors
- washing windows, cleaning up spills
- carrying in supplies or groceries from the car
- dusting furniture and surfaces with a vinegar-and-water solution and cloth
- putting away materials from the sensory table
- sorting papers and project materials
- stacking and unstacking chairs or moving items out of the way for circle time
- being the identified door holder, line leader, lunch/hallway/bathroom/going-outside monitor

Some work tasks need descriptive names, such as *door holder, message taker,* or *first-aid monitor.* For children who are not yet reading, an identifying icon or picture to indicate the task will be important. Favorite work activities tend to be those where the children have clear and specific instructions as to how the task should be done and where there are observable outcomes—for example, the paint is washed away (Readdick and Douglas, 2000). Work assignment charts, "pick-one" baskets, or rotating charts can provide opportunities for everyone to have a choice or be assigned work tasks.

Giving children the opportunity to work in pairs is also an option when the tasks can be done in true collaboration. Children should have the option to rotate and complete as many work

assignments as possible, and the teacher should keep a record of the tasks each child completes. To make work responsibilities more important to the classroom culture, consider designating a "classroom work" day. Having a special day just for classroom work elevates these experiences beyond the routines of everyday chores. Keeping a record of their work during the school year provides children acknowledgement that they can add to their portfolio of accomplishments. Avoid rewards such as stars, stickers, or "worker of the week" status. Children have limited recall memory, and they often miss opportunities to understand their impact unless adults take a bit of time to remember for them. It is amazing to see children's responses when they see their "List of Things I Did" at the end of a year!

Strengthening children's competencies for observation, problem solving, and making a contribution supports their capacity for resilience. For children who are missing pieces in their catalogues of competence, seeing and hearing with greater sensitivity and clarity, making decisions with less anxiety over whether the decision might be right or wrong, and knowing they are real contributors to the group does build the link between resilience and protective factors. Protective factors, which are external to the child, can be supported when children are better able to engage with their physical environment and participate with a realistic degree of self-assurance (Hodas, 2006; Werner, 1990). If children are aware of their skills and know within themselves that they have abilities and strategies that can be demonstrated, this knowledge can offset the negative, self-fulfilling expectation of rejection based on an emerging negative self-image that children who experience stress and trauma often have (Gartrell, 2012).

Ideas for Practice

The list that follows contains eight categories of skills, abilities, talents, aptitudes, and unique gifts that can be used to help children build a portfolio of competencies. The intent of the list is to generate creative ideas for the competencies that children may possess but rarely have acknowledged. It is not a matter of how well such abilities are done but the fact that they are present. For each category, think about how many items you could list for an individual child or for all the children in your classroom.

The examples are child initiated, taken from first-person interviews with three- and five-year-olds. They are limited by the children's perspective and self-awareness but can be one way to help children develop a more complete understanding of their capabilities. Adult comments can be added or given in place of those generated by children. Be creative in how you share such great information with the children: scrapbook, letter, computer file, or CD—the options are endless!

AREAS OF COMPETENCE

1. Things I can do to care for myself (hygiene and self-care):
   - fasten shoes
   - button clothes
   - wash face
   - brush teeth
   - wash hands
   - put on adhesive bandages

2. Things I know about myself:
   - I like pizza.
   - I like to play checkers.
   - I like video games.
   - I love my mom.
   - I'm going to Dad's if Jen is not there.

3. Things I know about other people:
   - My dad likes racing cars.
   - Mrs. Johnson has two kids.
   - Trey always goes to soccer.

4. Things I can do to care for other people:
   - open doors
   - get juice for the baby
   - carry in things from the car
   - hold Mom's cell phone

5. Things I know about the world:
   - You take the bus to go downtown but can't go by yourself.
   - You need a ticket for movies.

6. Things I can do to help out at school:
   - empty lunch trays
   - dust the whiteboards
   - close the bathroom door
   - not scream inside

7. Things I know about and from school:
   - I can count to 50.
   - I can play outside if I do not shove.
   - Bugs die.
   - Be quiet so you can think.
8. Things I know how to do that are special or that no one else can do:
   - hold my breath for 15 seconds
   - bake a cake
   - sing rap
   - wear cowgirl boots

Using Literature to
Support Children

FIVE THINGS WE KNOW

 Strengthening self-regulation and building competence are two key elements in building resilience for stress-affected children.

❷ Self-regulation involves not only managing impulsive behaviors but also attending to subtle physical and social cues that provide additional signals for better understanding one's physical and social world.

❸ Building three skills for self-regulation—body-sensory balance, awareness and sensory sensitivity, and the body-brain connection—can increase a child's physical and intellectual skills.

❹ Stress and trauma can have a damaging effect not only on the child's physical body and reactions but also on his feelings of ability, value to others, and self-worth.

❺ A child's awareness of his capabilities and importance to others are critical building blocks for developing authentic self-competence.

Traditional and Specialized Children's Literature

Reading to children, exploring books with them, and offering opportunities for children to explore books on their own provides a myriad of benefits:

- offering pleasure and sparking interest;
- recognizing and identifying prosocial values such as kindness, concern, sharing, and respect;
- presenting intellectual challenge;
- offering ways to connect personal experience;
- building early literacy skills, including vocabulary and word use;
- becoming informed about experiences they may not have had;
- creating a sense of shared community with others who are reading the same book;
- being exposed to varied and beautiful art work through book illustrations;
- constructing a common ground for shared vocabulary and concepts; and
- making connections between story content and higher-order learning in areas such as math and science.

As most early childhood professionals know, children's literature is vast and ever evolving. Typically, early childhood programs have book collections that include board books for very young children, early readers for those with emerging literacy skills, and chapter books for adults to read aloud or for children who can read on their own. Collections might include picture books; poetry; number and letter books; fiction, including folktales, fairy tales, and culturally specific legends; and nonfiction books that provide information on a wide variety of topics. Reading high-quality children's literature has enormous benefits for children. Avoid books that are focused on characters or stories from TV shows, movies, and cartoons.

While the focus of the literacy movement over the last 20 years has been on helping children acquire early reading skills, many books for young children also address complex social themes or topics (Jalongo, 2004). Books specifically focusing on a topic such as divorce or going to kindergarten, as well as those that concentrate on specific social or emotional skills such as managing anger or handling fear, are a significant part of most early childhood book collections. These books help children understand, identify with, and manage complex social and emotional issues and are unique, as they often combine a fictional story with information on a specific concept, such as sharing, caring for friends, or understanding illness.

Using Books to Assist Children in Understanding

Bibliotherapy is the practice of using literature to help people solve problems; think about different options and possible actions; and understand the feelings, perspectives, and ideas of others. People often identify with others through the experiences described in a book. When a book draws attention to social issues that are relevant to the experiences of young children, it offers a means of understanding in a way that is less intimidating than having a classroom discussion or lesson on the topic.

Specialized books address any number of behaviors, situations, events, or problems that might be easily identified as stress themed: parental separation; divorce; incarceration; deployment; hospitalization; death; serious or long-term illness; managing feelings of worry, fear, anger, and loneliness; and understanding homelessness, poverty, aspects of diversity, inclusion, and social acceptance. These books can provide ways for children to identify with, understand, and appreciate complex issues.

We know that children's exposure to and involvement with quality literature and the ways in which books and stories are communicated adds significant value to their intellectual and social-emotional development (Jalongo, 2004; Sutherland, 1997; Zeece, 2000, 2001). Jalongo cites the work of Lilian Katz, who identified four kinds of learning essential to the education of young children:

- knowledge,
- disposition,
- skills, and
- feelings.

These kinds of learning help bring attention to the need for a holistic and authentic approach to children's learning. Acquiring *knowledge* means learning concepts, facts, and ideas as well as social stories and legends common to one's culture. *Dispositions* are "habits of action" or ways of interacting with the world, often referred to as personality traits. Dispositions are both genetic and learned behaviors and may be constructive for interacting with the world—curiosity, creativity, independence, and responsibility—or less useful for interacting—selfishness, aggression, or disinterest. *Skills* are focused actions that are easily observed and change over time. Skills are not limited to physical abilities, such as cutting with scissors or riding a bicycle, but also include academic competencies, such as knowing letters and numbers and how to use them, and social capabilities, such as taking turns or communicating effectively with others. Learning about *feelings* centers on aspects of emotional competency—the awareness, identification, and management of emotional states within oneself and in interaction with others. These four critical dimensions apply to all areas of learning as children grow and develop, and may be well supported by appropriate literacy experiences (Katz and Chard, 1989).

Children's experiences with literature can foster and support all of the essential and interrelated types of learning. Jalongo cites what she calls the *iceberg principle:* "Dispositions and feelings make up the substantial portion that lies beneath the surface." Knowledge and skills are more visible, but the emotional understanding and awareness for children takes on a less visible, more thoughtful position.

Zeece, in her two-part series for *Early Childhood Education Journal*, "Meeting Children's Needs with Quality Literature," cites the work of Sutherland in outlining some of the basic needs

Helping Them Heal

children have that can be met through their experiences with books. These include the need for security, to love and to be loved, to belong, to achieve, to experience change, to know about the world, and to experience beauty and order. Books can provide children with ways to better understand themselves and their interactions with the world. Well-crafted stories also provide an opportunity for children to increase their skills in interacting with others and to identify and clarify ideas or experiences with which they have little or somewhat distorted experience. In addition, for children who may be new to mainstream American society, stories can also provide a means of better understanding the social

customs, expectations, and ways of managing challenges that are typical within mainstream culture (Akrofi et al., 2008).

One reason for including literature that has a very intentional focus, such as understanding the process of family connection despite separation or divorce or knowing how natural disasters affect many different kinds of people in different ways, is to assist children in developing perspective taking. Being able to understand what other people think, feel, know, and how they behave is a long developmental process and is closely linked with changes in cognitive development and experience (Bredekamp, 2010; Bredekamp and Copple; 2009; Curtis and Carter, 2003). The role of adults in expanding children's limited perspective taking, which is appropriately self-focused and egocentric, is to provide alternatives through modeling, clarification of errors and misunderstandings, and stories that build on familiar experiences. Expanded perspective taking allows children to better understand not only their own experiences—especially those that are inherently complex—but also those of others.

Quality children's literature can help children understand relationships and management of emotions in a variety of ways (Roberts and Crawford, 2008; Zeece, 2000):

- exploring values and beliefs of their own families and culture,
- learning that others have emotions similar to their own,
- exploring and identifying expressions of feelings and emotions,
- connecting with and learning from lives and experiences of others,
- increasing awareness of differences and similarities among people,
- seeing different options for communication with others, and
- honoring children's questions and perspectives (no matter how "inaccurate").

UNDERSTANDING *AT RISK*

Understanding the needs of at-risk children is an important responsibility for all early childhood educators. We often associate terms such as *disadvantaged* and *at risk* with less-than-optimal social and intellectual conditions and resulting negative outcomes, especially behavior. Taking a deficit perspective means seeing children, including those who experience stress and trauma, as having more negative qualities than positive or constructive qualities, especially when it comes to their experience with literature (Volk and Long, 2005). Many children who experience disadvantaged early childhood environments are exposed to a multitude of literacy-rich but perhaps nontraditional experiences, such as environmental print, commercially produced comic books, and multilingual magazines. Early childhood classrooms that include high-quality children's literature provide opportunities for children who are affected by stress and trauma to extend their understanding and have their personal experiences validated.

For many children, having good experiences with literature becomes an association of support. They acquire positive feelings through the process of reading and being read to. By identifying with story content, they may also feel warmth, closeness, reassurance, and identity (Zeece, 2000). In addition, exposure to subjects that are complex and linked with strong emotions in the form of a story can provide children with a way to understand both the event and the feelings as somewhat separate occurrences. Experiences with well-crafted, authentic literature can help children not only acquire factual information, emotional comfort, and social support, but also exposure to constructive models for coping with stress, anxiety, fear, and worry (Roberts and Crawford, 2008). When major events occur, such as violence in a community, damaging storms, or fires, stories that provide developmentally appropriate information can help offset distortions that children may have and provide a way for them to understand not only events but also how others respond and cope with these events (Zeece, 1998).

While the stressed child may be the focus for using specialized literature as a learning and therapeutic tool, it is important to remember that the less-stressed child is also a beneficiary. Quality children's books can increase the awareness, understanding, and empathy of children who have less direct experience with trauma, separation, loss, and stress.

Ideas for Implementing Literature Experiences

When teachers appropriately use literature to address stress-themed topics, most children will experience a sense of being in a safety zone for learning and identifying with story content (Zeece and Stolzer, 2002). Story content that focuses on physical and emotional safety, reassurance, predictability, moving ahead, and appropriate emotional responses can help children regain a sense of balance.

Introducing these specialized literature experiences does require a bit of planning and reflection. Suggestions for choosing stories and class readings about stress-themed topics include the following (Jalongo, 2004; Roberts and Crawford, 2008; Zeece, 2000, 2001):

1. Review the book content and presentation, illustrations, and so on prior to placing the book in the classroom and reading with the children. Be sure to look for appropriate, culturally respectful, and relevant illustrations, word use, gender typing, and problem resolution. Will the book be useful and helpful for a child who is sad, lonely, worried, or anxious? Are the characters ones with whom the children can identify? Is the story line believable without being too preachy or overly sweet? Are the adults portrayed as supportive, caring, and also realistic? Are the images accurate or are they too scary or poorly drawn?

2. Introduce the book topic and perhaps the name and gender of the main character before reading the book to the children. For example, let the children know that a book about homelessness is one that you will be reading for circle time tomorrow. Talk about what *homelessness* means.

3. Provide a brief review of the book prior to opening and reading the text. Let the children know you will be talking about the book after you have finished the story. If there are new vocabulary words, make sure the children have a clear understanding of the important terms that will be used in the story.

4. Read the story with confidence and ease as you would any other story for group time. After the story is complete, give a brief review of what the story was about, or ask open-ended questions such as these:

   ■ What is the story about?
   ■ How does the main character feel in the story?
   ■ What is your favorite part of the story?
   ■ What happens at the end of the story?
   ■ What do you think might happen next?
   ■ What character is your favorite?
   ■ Is there a character you do not like very much?
   ■ What new word(s) did you learn from the book?
   ■ What will you remember about this story tomorrow?
   ■ What about the story made you feel (happy, sad, afraid, angry, and so on)?

- What would you do if you were (character in the story)?
- If you could make up a new ending to the story, what would it be?
- If you told your (mom, dad, grandma, friend) about this story, what would you say?

5. Questions and follow-up experiences related to the story can include activities such as the following:
   - retelling the story to others
   - drawing a picture based on ideas or events in the book
   - re-enacting an event from the story as part of dramatic play
   - making or dictating a list of questions to be answered by the teacher or even addressed to the author
   - making a "feel better" art project for a main character (if appropriate)
   - having children create a similar book with their own illustrations and story line

6. See more suggestions on classroom implementation in the Ideas for Practice section at the end of this chapter.

CAUTION: HANDLE WITH CARE

When addressing a sensitive topic such as divorce, homelessness, parental incarceration, or separation, proceed with extreme care. Before discussing with the group what may be a personal issue for a child in your class, talk with the child and make sure that the topic will not be too upsetting or embarrassing. Be sure to keep all confidential information private.

One of the most important components of an early childhood program is the inclusion of literature and reading experiences that enhance and expand the intellectual and social experiences of young children. Including books and literature experiences that address stress-themed topics is one way to provide support, validation, and understanding for both stress-affected and nonaffected children. Creating emotionally safe opportunities in which children can see visual images through book illustrations, talk about stressful experiences, and talk about how people cope with these events is important for building resilience skills and capacity. Roberts and Crawford (2008) note that "real life does indeed call for real books, books that provide information,

comfort, and models for coping with life's difficult times."
Literature experiences can highlight and support positive
interactions and understanding between children and their
teachers and other significant adults and can build a foundation of
trust when children's perception, skills, and feelings are honored
and respected (Zeece, 2001).

Appendix B offers an annotated list of books for preschool and
young school-age children. These books were selected for their
developmentally appropriate content, illustrations, and story
line. The topics cover a number of situations, events, emotions,
and stressful situations that impact children who have significant
stress experience as well as those who have much less.

Ideas for Practice

The following resources offer more information on selecting children's books, implementing book-themed ideas in the classroom, and engaging parents. You may also want to look at the Reading Chair section of *Young Children*, published by NAEYC. You can also find excellent book reviews and ideas for classroom practice in the *Early Childhood Education Journal;* see the Books for Children reviews, especially those by Pauline Davey Zeece. Publications by Bruce and Cairone (2011), Landy (2002), and Wheeler (2004) also contain lists of stress-themed books.

Selecting Children's Literature

- The American Library Association provides extensive annotated book lists for children of all ages at www.ala.org/alsc/booklists.
- The children's book committee at the Bank Street College of Education selects and provides reviews on the best books for children published each year. Each book accepted for the list is read and reviewed by at least two committee members and is then discussed by the committee as a whole. See http://bankstreet.edu/center-childrens-literature/childrens-book-committee.
- Teachers First is a collection of lessons, units, and web resources designed to assist classroom teachers, especially kindergarten and first grade professionals. See www.teachersfirst.com/100books.cfm.
- The Children's Book Council is a national nonprofit trade association of children's book publishers. The council sponsors Children's Book Week, a celebration of books and reading since 1919 and the nation's longest-running literacy initiative. The council also provides reviewed book lists organized by age and genre at www.cbcbooks.org/readinglists.php.
- Reading Rockets is a national multimedia literacy initiative sponsored by the U.S. Department of Education that offers information and resources on how to help young children up to age nine learn to read. The initiative's website includes book lists reviewed by teachers for children, child-reviewed lists, and classroom strategies for promoting emergent and foundational

literacy and working with families. Reading Rockets' book lists are located at www.readingrockets.org/books/booksbytheme/.

Implementing Literacy Practices

- *The Boy Who Would Be a Helicopter* by Vivian Paley
- *The Girl with the Brown Crayon: How Children Use Stories to Shape Their Lives* by Vivian Paley
- *The Story S-T-R-E-T-C-H-E-R-S* series by Shirley C. Raines and Robert J. Canady
- *Using Caldecotts Across the Curriculum* by Joan Novelli

Appendix A:
Life Stress Scale
(Sources of Childhood Stress*)

Stress or Change	Value	Score
Parent dies	100	
Parents divorce	73	
Parents separate	65	
Separation from parent (foster placement, termination of parental rights, child raised by relatives)	65	
Parent travels for work	63	
Close family member dies	63	
Personal injury, abuse, or illness	53	
Parent remarries	50	
Parent loses job	47	
Separated parents reconcile	45	
Mother starts job outside of home	45	
Change in health of a family member	44	
Mother becomes pregnant	40	
School difficulties	39	
Birth of a sibling	39	
School readjustment (new teacher or class)	39	
Change in family"s financial condition	38	
Injury or illness of a close friend	37	
Starts or changes extracurricular activity (for example, music lessons, sport)	36	
Change in number of fights with sibling(s)	35	
Exposed to violence at school	31	
Theft of personal possessions	30	
Change in responsibility at home	29	

Stress or Change	Value	Score
Older sibling leaves home	29	
Trouble with grandparents	29	
Outstanding personal achievement	28	
Move to another city	26	
Move to another part of town	26	
New pet or loss of pet	25	
Change in personal habits	24	
Trouble with teacher	24	
Change in time with babysitter or at child care	20	
Change to new school	20	
Change in play habits	19	
Vacation with family	19	
Change in friends	18	
Attending summer camp	17	
Change in sleeping habits	16	
Change in number of family get-togethers	15	
Change in eating habits	15	
Change in amounts of television viewing	13	
Birthday party	12	
Punishment for "not telling the truth"	11	
* Adapted from Holmes and Rahe (1967) and Foxman (2004)		

Other stress events that are often listed for children (usually of school age):

- Going blind/deaf
- Being kept in the same grade next year
- Wetting pants in class
- Hearing parents quarrel or fight
- Being caught stealing something
- Telling the truth and no one believing
- Getting a bad progress report or report card
- Being sent to the principal's office
- Getting lost in a strange place
- Being laughed at
- Being bullied
- Having a scary dream
- Being picked last for a team
- Not being asked to a party

(Source: Yamamoto and Byrnes, 1987)

Appendix B: Annotated Resources

for Teachers, Families, and Children

Bibliography of Children's Books

Adoption

Carlson, Nancy. 2006. *My Family is Forever*. New York: Puffin.

> This book about the experience of being adopted is written in a child's language. The author touches on the different ways families are formed and how adopted children may look different but be terrific just the same.

Curtis, Jamie Lee. 1996. *Tell Me Again about the Night I Was Born*. New York: HarperCollins.

> This humor-filled book looks at an adopted girl's birth experience, which she remembers through the words of her mother and father. She knows the story by heart and delights in hearing it again and again. A sincere story about the making of a family.

Fry, Ying Ying. 2001. *Kids Like Me in China*. St. Paul, MN: Yeong and Yeong.

> This book is a simple depiction of adoption told through the eyes of a child adopted from China. The author addresses the complex feelings of one child's journey as she contemplates what her early life in an orphanage may have been like.

Lewis, Rose. 2000. *I Love You Like Crazy Cakes*. New York: Little, Brown.

> *I Love You Like Crazy Cakes* discusses the airplane ride, life in the orphanage, and the homecoming of the new baby as it recounts one mother's trip to China to adopt a baby.

Richmond, Marianne. 2008. *I Wished for You: An Adoption Story*. Naperville, IL: Sourcebooks.

> A touching story in which a mama and adopted little bear talk about adoption and how much they love each other.

Stoeke, Janet. 2005. *Waiting for May*. New York: Puffin.

This book follows one family's long wait to meet their adopted child. Simple explanations are given to a curious child who has lots of questions about his new sister and her journey from China.

Alternative Family Structures: Gay and Lesbian Parenting

Merchant, Ed. 2010. *Dad David, Baba Chris, and Me*. London: British Association for Adoption and Fostering.

The author provides a story of two dads who love their son and each other.

Oelschlager, Vanita. 2011. *A Tale of Two Mommies*. Akron, OH: Vanita Books.

This story offers a simple yet informative portrayal of questions commonly asked about a child who lives in a same-sex parent household.

Anger

Agassi, Martine. 2009. *Hands Are Not for Hitting*. Minneapolis, MN: Free Spirit.

This book offers children positive alternatives to hitting and hurtful behavior. It looks at constructive ways of coping with and resolving strong feelings, including anger, jealousy, and fear.

Bang, Molly. 1999. *When Sophie Gets Angry—Really, Really Angry*. New York: Scholastic.

The content addresses appropriate ways to deal with anger and helps children realize that everyone gets angry sometimes.

Hoose, Phillip. 1998. *Hey, Little Ant*. New York: Scholastic.

A little boy considers whether or not to squish an insignificant ant, but then discovers the ant can talk. A lively discussion between two unlikely characters addresses the topic of remembering that everyone is different, but everyone has feelings.

Lichetenheld, Tom. 2003. *What Are You So Grumpy About?* New York: Little, Brown.

A funny story about dealing with the feelings of grumpiness. Each idea offers children ways to get in touch with their feelings and ways to cope.

Meiners, Cheri. 2010. *Cool Down and Work through Anger* (Learning to Get Along). Minneapolis, MN: Free Spirit.

This book helps children to understand and work through their anger. It supports the concept that it is normal to feel angry but important to express anger in a safe way.

Moses, Brian. 1993. *I Feel Angry (Your Feelings)*. Hove, East Sussex, UK: Wayland.

This book offers various humorous solutions to manage anger. The author's creative illustrations of what anger may "look" like are most appropriate for young children.

Nickle, John. 1999. *The Ant Bully*. New York: Scholastic.

Lucas vents his anger at being bullied on defenseless ants but soon finds out that even ants can fight back.

Rosenthal, Amy. 2008. *It's Not Fair!* New York: HarperCollins.

Rosenthal reassures preschool readers that everyone feels the same way at some point. Even pigs, planets, and square pegs can relate, because their lives are not fair either.

Anxiety or Fear

Beguley, Elizabeth. 2011. *Ready Steady Ghost!* Great Clarendon, Oxford, UK: Oxford University Press.

This book is about one little ghost who feels afraid of the big scary forest. The author explores children's feelings about being little in a huge world. This story offers reassurance that you can find your place in the world and do big things.

Bosschaert, Greet. 2001. *Teenie Bird: And How She Learned to Fly*. New York: Harry N. Abrams.

A tiny starling hesitates to learn to fly like her big brothers before her. The story touches on a familiar fear that many children have when they venture out of their safety zone and experience new things.

Browne, Anthony. 2007. *Silly Billy*. Cambridge, MA: Candlewick.

Billy is a boy who worries a lot. Most of all, he worries about staying at other people's houses. A visit to his grandma's house offers him a delightful solution; using his imagination, and with the help of a tiny worry doll, he learns to deal with his fear.

Chriscoe, Sharon. 2008. *Scary Weather, Scaredy Cat*. Baltimore, MD: PublishAmerica.

Small children are often afraid of weather, especially when it involves loud noises or flashes of lightning. In this story, readers follow one boy's journey as he deals with his fear of lightning.

Clare Bell, Juliet. 2011. *Don't Panic, Annika!* London: Piccadilly Press.

Annika panics about the smallest things. This book explores the ways that Annika's family helps her handle life's small trials and offers ideas for learning to be calm.

Dunbar, Joyce. 1999. *Tell Me Something Happy Before I Go to Sleep.* San Diego, CA: Harcourt Brace.

A little girl has trouble falling asleep. Her brother knows just what she needs and suggests she think of something positive. This book offers creative ideas for calming bedtime anxiety and portrays a warm connection between siblings.

Dunn Buron, Kari. 2006. *When My Worries Get Too Big! a Relaxation Book for Kids Who Live with Anxiety.* Shawnee Mission, KS: Autism Asperger Publishing.

The little boy in the book offers a simple yet unique method he uses to deal with his anxious feelings. Parents can use this book to help their child work through anxious feelings and explore useful relaxation techniques.

Durant, Alan. 2008. *Billy Monster's Daymare.* Wilton, CT: Tiger Tales.

This book explores a common nighttime fear: monsters under the bed. As children read about one monster's "daymare" and his fear of a child during the day, they can connect their own nighttime fears with this story.

Dutro, Jack. 1993. *Night Light: A Story for Children Afraid of the Dark.* Milwaukee, WI: G. Stevens.

The author helps children use their imaginations to change their perception of scary things into images of fun and comfort.

Freedman, Claire. 2012. *Tappity-Tap! What Was That?* London: Scholastic.

Owl, Mouse, and Rabbit hear a strange noise outside. They tremble, fearing it might be the monster of the woods. They soon realize their fearsome monster is more fuzzy than scary and that most things are not quite as scary as they seem.

Gliori, Debi. 1999. *No Matter What.* San Diego, CA: Harcourt Brace.

This book may offer an anxious or insecure child reassurance that "no matter what" their parents love them unconditionally. It reinforces the message that love carries on even after the death of a loved one.

Gravett, Emily. 2008. *Little Mouse's Big Book of Fears.* New York: Simon and Schuster Books for Young Readers.

This book follows one tiny mouse who is very fearful. The takeaway message is that fears must be faced in order to be defeated. The author provides space for children to write down their feelings and fears in a journal-like fashion.

Guanci, Anne Marie. 2007. *David and the Worry Beast: Helping Children Cope with Anxiety*. Far Hills, NJ: New Horizon Press.

This book helps children conquer their fears and deal with anxiety. Everyone worries, but when those worries get in the way of happy, it is important to find ways to cope.

Ironside, Virginia. 2004. *The Huge Bag of Worries*. London: HodderWayman.

In this story, Jenny's worries follow her in a big blue bag. This book provides an opportunity for children to talk about their worries and to let them go, as Jenny learns to do.

Lewis, Paeony. 2008. *I'll Always Love You*. Wilton, CT: Tiger Tales.

Alex Bear has been naughty, but he finds out he is loved no matter what he does. This book offers a gentle example of unconditional love that a parent has toward a child, even when the child makes mistakes.

Lite, Lori. 1996. *A Boy and a Bear: The Children's Relaxation Book*. Plantation, FL: Specialty Press.

A boy and a bear befriend each other and learn important lessons in relaxation. The bear watches the boy breathe while the reader mirrors these techniques to enhance her own relaxation skills.

Lite, Lori. 2008a. *Angry Octopus: An Anger Management Story*. Marietta, GA: Litebooks.Net

Children get angry and anxious; this book helps them explore how anger "feels" in their bodies and offers a practical physical approach to managing anger and anxiety through mind and body awareness.

Lite, Lori. 2008b. *Sea Otter Cove: A Relaxation Story*. Marietta, GA: Litebooks.Net

An audiobook providing 60 minutes of relaxation and stress management. Children explore with different sea animals and learn breathing techniques as well as visualization.

Meade, Holly. 2011. *If I Never Forever Endeavor*. Somerville, MA: Candlewick.

One little bird is scared to venture beyond his nest and worries about all of the "what ifs" if he leaves. He soon learns that he will not be able to do anything if he does not at least try.

Meadows, Michelle. 2003. *The Way the Storm Stops*. New York: Henry Holt.

Simple story line and illustrations frame an age-old story of one mother comforting her child through the lights and sounds of a scary thunderstorm. The text offers a singsong pattern to the sounds and escalation of a thunderstorm.

Moser, Adolph. 1988. *Don't Pop Your Cork on Mondays! The Children's Anti-Stress Book*. Kansas City, KS: Landmark Editions.

Moser addresses the effects of stress and the causes. Using humor, he illustrates how to help children recognize stress in their bodies and use appropriate techniques to manage it.

Moses, Brian. 1993. *I Feel Frightened*. East Sussex, UK: Wayland.

This imaginative book explores children's fears of everyday events and the coping strategies they use to deal with ordinary fears.

Moses, Brian. 1997. *I'm Worried*. East Sussex, UK: Wayland.

This book helps describe feelings of anxiety that some children may experience and provides solutions to help them deal with this emotion, with helpful notes for parents and caregivers.

Smith, Alex. 2010. *Bella and Monty: A Hairy, Scary Night*. London: Hodder and Stoughton.

Monty is scared of just about everything, and his best friend, Bella, helps him to overcome his fears. This book provides an opportunity for children to learn about their own fears and what other people fear as well.

Stimson, Joan. 1994. *Worried Arthur*. Loughborough, UK: Ladybird.

Arthur the penguin worries about everything, especially about Christmas. Arthur's dad offers him reassurance, and as Christmas morning arrives, Arthur has stopped worrying and delights when he realizes that Santa found his house.

Thomas, Pat. 2010. *Why Do I Feel Scared? A First Look at Being Brave*. Hauppauge, NY: Barron's.

In this book children discover that there are many ways to be brave and that they can involve doing the right thing when it is difficult. The author encourages children to face challenges and realize that being brave may not always be easy, but it is empowering.

Uff, Caroline. 2007. *The Worry Monster*. London: Orchard.

This story is about one little girl whose dog was punished for wrongdoing, when she herself was responsible. Throughout the book, the little girl is plagued with worry and guilt that continues to grow. She realizes that if she talks about her worry, it goes away a lot faster.

Viorst, Judith 1973. *My Mama Says There Aren't Any Zombies, Ghosts, Vampires, Creatures, Demons, Monsters, Fiends, Goblins, or Things.* New York: Atheneum.

This book offers a unique perspective about a child who wonders if he can trust his mom when she explains there are no monsters. He comes to trust his mom when he is afraid of the dark at night and she comforts him.

Viorst, Judith. 1988. *The Good-Bye Book.* New York: Atheneum.

The author presents a little boy's attempts to thwart his parents leaving him with a babysitter for the night. This book may be useful to parents who have ever experienced difficulties in trying to separate from their children for an evening.

Willis, Jeanine. 2012. *Fly, Chick, Fly!* Minneapolis, MN: Andersen Press.

Fly, Chick, Fly! represents the anxiety and worry every child feels while growing up. This book shows children the importance of managing fear, instead of letting it hold them back.

Wolff, Ferida. 2005. *Is a Worry Worrying You?* Terre Haute, IN: Tanglewood Press.

This book recognizes that life is stressful, even for small children who worry a lot. The author uses humor and provides options for children to learn creative problem solving.

Coping with Siblings

Kopelke, Lisa. 2006. *The Younger Brother's Survival Guide.* New York: Simon and Schuster.

Matt shares his tips on how to avoid the perils that being the younger sibling brings, including lessons on why you should not run around the house in your underwear. The book's humor helps children learn effective ways to deal with sibling rivalry.

Death

Brown, Margaret. 1935. *The Dead Bird.* New York: Morrow.

Children find a small, still-warm but dying bird. They decide to give the bird a proper burial and visit it every day. This book gives naturally curious children a touching and simple perspective about death.

Erlbruch, Wolf. 2011. *Duck, Death, and the Tulip.* Wellington, NZ: Gecko Press.

Duck works through his fear of death. He learns to better understand his fears and what it means to face death in a child-appropriate way.

Harris, Robbie. 2004. *Goodbye, Mousie.* New York: Aladdin.

A little boy wakes up one day to find that his pet mouse will not wake up. Readers learn about death in simple, easily understood language.

Joosse, Barbara. 2001. *Ghost Wings*. San Francisco, CA: Chronicle Books.

> When her grandma becomes ill and dies, a little girl learns from her grandpa that the people she loves are not gone forever; they live on in her heart and memories.

Kaplow, Julie, and Pincus, Donna. 2007. *Samantha Jane's Missing Smile: A Story about Coping with the Loss of a Parent*. Washington, DC: Magination Press.

> This story follows one little girl on her journey of grieving the loss of her father. It also addresses questions and worries that children may have about death. The book stresses the concept that parents want their children to live happy and full lives.

Mundy, Michaelene. 2009. *What Happens When Someone Dies?* St. Meinrad, IN: One Caring Place.

> This book helps explain to children what happens after people die, taking them through the funeral process and helping them to say goodbye. The story offers a poignant look at one child's experience with the death of his grandfather.

Olivieri, Laura. 2007. *Where Are You? A Child's Book about Loss*. Lulu.com.

> Designed to help children of all ages deal with the loss of a loved one, *Where Are You? A Child's Book about Loss* provides comfort to young children and eases the stress of grieving.

Thomas, Pat. 2001. *I Miss You: A First Look at Death*. Hauppauge, NY: Barron's.

> *I Miss You* explains that death can come in many different forms and can occur at different ages.

Wilhelm, Hans. 1988. *I'll Always Love You*. Albuquerque, NM: Dragonfly.

> A little boy loses his beloved dog. The family has a burial and helps the boy learn about unconditional love even when something we love is gone.

Developmental Differences

Andreae, Giles. 2001. *Giraffes Can't Dance*. New York: Orchard.

> The author helps insecure young readers realize their potential to be great, even if they march to a different beat. A clumsy giraffe named Gerald is befriended by a cricket that helps him find a way to achieve his desire to learn to dance.

Fleming, Virginia. 1993. *Be Good to Eddie Lee*. New York: Philomel.

> This book explores one girl's discovery of friendship as she spends time with a neighbor boy who has Down syndrome. This story accurately depicts the attitudes and behavior typically displayed by children when it comes to their interactions with children who are differently abled.

Glenn, Sharlee. 2004. *Keeping Up with Roo*. New York: Putnam.

> A story about a young girl whose best friend is her mentally challenged aunt. As she grows older, she realizes that her aunt has special needs and worries what her friends will think. Ultimately she realizes how capable her aunt is.

Kraus, Robert. 1994. *Leo the Late Bloomer*. New York: HarperCollins.

> Leo the tiger struggles to accomplish tasks that others can already do. He works through being discouraged and continuing to try, even when things seem impossible.

Lears, Laurie. 1998. *Ian's Walk: A Story about Autism*. Morton Grove, IL: Albert Whitman.

> *Ian's Walk* conveys the complexity of having a child with autism and how one family copes. It takes her brother, Ian, being lost in the park for a young girl to realize how much she cares about him.

Meyer, Donald. 1997. *Views from our Shoes: Growing up with a Brother or Sister with Special Needs*. Bethesda, MD: Woodbine House.

> For older children, this book is a collection of stories by children and young adults who have a sibling with a disability. Personal stories help the reader understand his own feelings.

Stuve-Bodeen, Stephanie. 1998. *We'll Paint the Octopus Red*. Bethesda, MD: Woodbine House.

> This book explores one family's experience of having a baby born with Down syndrome. Emma and her father help each other to realize that Isaac is precious and wanted no matter what special needs he may have.

Divorce/Visitation

Franz Ransom, Jeannie. 2000. *I Don't Want to Talk about It*. Washington, DC: Magination Press.

> This book discusses the sadness and anger children feel when they are told their parents are getting a divorce. It addresses the issues and feelings that children are often reluctant to talk about and the importance of parents being supportive.

Lansky, Vicki. 1997. *It's Not Your Fault, KoKo Bear*. Minnetonka, MN: Book Peddlers.

> This book guides young children through first hearing the word *divorce* by working through the questions that may come up during the process. It helps children to understand how their family life will change and gives them the opportunity to identify their feelings.

Levins, Sandra. 2005. *Was It the Chocolate Pudding? A Story for Little Kids about Divorce.* Washington, DC: Magination Press.

Levins takes the complex vocabulary used by adults and translates it into terms a child can understand. The book emphasizes that divorce is not the child's fault. It deals with practical day-to-day matters surrounding divorce, separation, and visitation.

Masurel, Claire. 2003. *Two Homes.* Cambridge, MA: Candlewick.

Even when he must live in two homes, the main character finds that there are good things about both. He also is reminded by both parents, each day, how much he is loved.

Schmitz, Tamara. 2008. *Standing on My Own Two Feet: A Child's Affirmation of Love in the Midst of Divorce.* New York: Penguin.

The author uses repetition to drive home the important message that children are loved even when their parents divorce. One main character works through his feelings about the divorce, comes to terms with the finality of the situation, and realizes that the divorce was not his fault.

Thomas, Pat. 1998. *My Family Is Changing.* Hauppauge, NY: Barron's.

This book talks frankly about the many issues of divorce that children may face, including separation, divided custody, sorrow, loss, and anger.

Feelings

Anholt, Catherine. 1995. *What Makes Me Happy?* Cambridge MA: Candlewick.

This simple book explores the concept of feelings as told by children themselves. The story touches on feelings that may be difficult to define and express.

Cain, Janan. 2004. *The Way I Feel.* Seattle, WA: Parenting Press.

The Way I Feel explores emotions that preschool children may experience and helps put the feelings into words. This book is particularly helpful for children who may struggle to express their feelings.

McCourt, Lisa. 2004. *I Love You, Stinky Face.* New York: Scholastic.

A little boy delays bedtime with his many, many questions for his mom. He imagines himself as many different things, each time asking for reassurance that his mother will love him no matter what.

Munsch, Robert. 1995. *Love You Forever.* Scarborough, Ontario: Firefly.

Love You Forever helps children to understand that no matter how many mistakes they make, they will always be loved.

Parr, Todd. 2009. *The Feelings Book.* New York: Hachette.

The author takes an unusual approach to getting in touch with feelings. Appropriate for preschoolers, the book is well illustrated and funny to read.

Safran, Sheri. 2006. *All Kinds of Fears*. London: Tango Books.

The author covers a wide range of fears that most children experience. The central message tells children that it is okay to be afraid sometimes but discusses the importance of talking about fears in order to understand them.

Safran, Sheri. 2004. *All Kinds of Feelings*. London: Tango.

This book explores a range of feelings, discusses the importance of expressing feelings, and offers ideas about how to cope.

Viorst, Judith. 1987. *Alexander and the Terrible, Horrible, No Good, Very Bad Day*. New York: Aladdin.

The author follows Alexander on his journey through a bad day and explains that everyone has days like these. This book offers children a glimpse into what someone else may feel like on a bad day and helps them cope with their own very bad day.

Foster Care and Out-of-Home Placements

Gillman, Jan. 2008. *Murphy's Three Homes: A Story for Children in Foster Care*. Washington, DC: Magination Press.

Murphy is a young puppy who is moved from home to home and wonders what he did wrong to make no one want him—a familiar sentiment for many foster children. This book is especially helpful for young children who may not be capable of understanding the exact reason for their foster-home placement.

Levy, Janice. 2004. *Finding the Right Spot: When Kids Can't Live with Their Parents*. Washington, DC: Magination Press.

This book is written for children in out-of-home placement but not in foster care. It discusses the reasons why children may have to live with other relatives or adult friends until they can return home.

Nelson, Julie. 2006. *Families Change: A Book for Children Experiencing Termination of Parental Rights*. Minneapolis, MN: Free Spirit.

Nelson explores the difficult topic of foster-care placement with reassuring, simple language. The goal of the book is to help children understand that others may be in the same situation and offers reassurance that they are not responsible for the situation in which they find themselves.

Sambrooks, Paul. 2000. *Dennis Duckling*. London: Children's Society.

This book is especially useful for young children who are experiencing placement. It explores the feelings one little duck has as he is removed from his birth mom and dad and moved to a different pond where a new set of adults begins caring for him.

Wilgocki, Jennifer. 2002. *Maybe Days*. Washington, DC: Magination Press.

Maybe Days examines many of the issues a child may encounter as she enters the foster care system. It addresses the majority of questions that children may have and helps them understand some of the complex questions that may not always have answers.

Homelessness

Gunning, Monica. 2004. *A Shelter in Our Car*. San Francisco, CA: Children's Book Press.

This book chronicles a young girl's experience with homelessness. Homelessness is a reality for some children, and this book takes a serious look at one child's firsthand experiences.

Bunting, Eve. 1991. *Fly Away Home*. New York: Clarion Books.

A little boy lives with his father at the airport, the only "home" they have. This book explores issues of homelessness and invisibility to others as told through the eyes of a child.

Illness in the Family

Andrews, Beth. 2012. *Why Are You So Scared?* Washington, DC: Magination Press.

The author offers answers to questions young children may have when their parent has post-traumatic stress disorder. As many families experience deployment and other violence, children can find reassurance and understanding in this book's content.

Butler, Dori. 2007. *My Grandpa's Had a Stroke*. Washington, DC: Magination Press.

One boy's journey watching as his grandpa recovers from a stroke. The book uses simple language to explain a complex situation in ways that are appropriate for children.

Filligenzi, Courtney. 2009. *Let My Colors Out*. Atlanta, GA: American Cancer Society.

Let My Colors Out helps children who are facing their parent's serious illness. Content addresses a range of emotional responses and explains that these feelings are all normal and part of the healing process.

Jacobs Altman, Linda. 2002. *Singing with Momma Lou.* New York: Lee and Low.
Tamika visits her grandma, who has Alzheimer's, at the nursing home.
As grandma becomes unable to recognize her, Tamika is reluctant to visit.
Tamika decides to jog her grandma's memory, and they find a connection.

Langston, Laura. 2004. *Remember, Grandma?* New York: Penguin.
Margaret's grandma forgets a lot, and Margaret is determined to help
her grandma know how much she is loved regardless of how well she
remembers. This book explains dementia in simple terms, helping children
to work through their fears and confusion.

Schnurbush, Barbara. 2006. *Striped Shirts and Flowered Pants: A Story about
Alzheimer's Disease for Young Children.* Washington, DC: Magination Press.
Libby learns about her grandmother's illness with gentle reassurance and
support from her family. She begins to understand how her grandma will
change and discovers ways to cope with her feelings and concerns.

Incarceration of a Loved One

Brisson, Pat. 2004. *Mama Loves Me from Away.* Honesdale, PA: Boyds Mills.
This book explores a young child's feelings during weekly visitations with her
incarcerated mother. Her mom helps her to cope with her absence by giving
her a special gift to keep close while she is away.

Dyches, Richard. 2010. *Kofi's Mom.* Evans, GA: Children Left Behind, Inc.
Kofi is confused after his mom is sent to prison. He finds comfort as he talks
to his classmates and begins to look forward to her return home.

Higgins, Melissa. 2011. *The Night Dad Went to Jail.* Mankato, MN: Picture
Window Books.
The author offers answers to questions children may have about what
happens to a parent who is incarcerated. *The Night Dad Went to Jail* explains
the process of going to jail using simple terms and thoughtful illustrations.

Making and Keeping Friends

Choldenko, Gennifer. 2006. *How to Make Friends with a Giant.* New York: Putnam.
From Jake's perspective as the shortest kid in the class to Jacomo's
experience being the tallest, the two find common ground as they work
together to form an uncommon friendship.

Counsel, June. 1986. *But Martin!* London: Faber and Faber.
Four children head back to school expecting an ordinary day, but it all turns
upside down when they are visited by an alien named Martin. This story
focuses on what it is like to feel different and feeling anxious about going
back to school.

Dismondy, Maria. 2008. *Spaghetti in a Hot Dog Bun: Having the Courage to Be Who You Are*. Northville, MI: Ferne Press.

The author emphasizes the importance of being yourself. This book empowers children to do the right thing, even when others challenge you.

Dismondy, Maria. 2012. *Pink Tiara Cookies for Three*. Dearborn, MI: Making Spirits Bright.

In the story, Sami learns that she can keep her best friend but also make room for a new friend.

Gorbachev, Valeri. 2005. *That's What Friends Are For*. New York: Philomel.

Everyone needs a friend like Goat, especially when Pig is found crying. Goat thinks his friend needs help but discovers that it is merely onions that are making his friend tear up. The two believe in collaborative effort as they cut onions together, because that's what friends are for.

Meiners, Cheri. 2004. *Join in and Play*. Minneapolis, MN: Free Spirit.

Making friends and playing with others is fun but not always easy to do. This simple and informative book addresses how to make friends.

O'Neill, Alexis. 2002. *The Recess Queen*. New York: Scholastic.

Mean Jean is the recess bully, but she soon meets her match in little Katie Sue, who is not having any part of being pushed around. As children read about the creative behavior exhibited by Katie Sue, they identify the self-confidence needed to stand up to a bully.

Rodman, Mary. 2007. *My Best Friend*. New York: Viking.

Lily is determined to have Tamika as a best friend, but a problem arises when Tamika states she already has a best friend. This book captures the disappointment of one girl's desire to be best friends and how Lily chooses to handle the situation.

Silverstein, Shel. 1986. *The Giving Tree*. New York: HarperCollins.

Silverstein's story of unconditional love, loss, and sacrifice chronicles the relationship between a boy and a tree that spans a lifetime.

Tafuri, Nancy. 2000. *Will You Be My Friend? A Bunny and Bird Story*. New York: Scholastic.

A chance meeting between outgoing Bunny and shy Bird culminates in friendship.

Military Deployment

Bunting, Eve. 2005. *My Red Balloon*. Honesdale, PA: Boyds Mills Press.

My Red Balloon chronicles one small boy's experience of having his sailor daddy return from sea. The boy holds his red balloon as a signal so his father will know he is there. This book touches on the feelings of being reunited after a long separation.

Ehrmantraut, Brenda. 2005. *Night Catch*. Lansing, MI: Bubble Gum Press.

> Though stationed halfway around the world, one father finds an ingenious way to connect with his son with the help of the North Star.

McElroy, Lisa. 2005. *Love, Lizzie: Love Letters to a Military Mom*. Morton, IL: Albert Whitman.

> A little girl copes with her mother's deployment overseas. This book also offers suggestions for families about how to deal with military deployment, including answers to the why questions that children inevitably ask.

Pelton, Mindy. 2004. *When Dad's at Sea*. Morton Grove, IL: Albert Whitman.

> This beautifully illustrated book captures one child's approach for coping with and being supported during the long absence of her father, a Navy pilot.

Tomp, Sarah. 2005. *Red, White, and Blue Good-bye*. New York: Walker.

> A young girl expresses her unhappiness with her father's departure to sea; at the same time her father helps her to cope. Her father takes her on outings before he goes and leaves her with reminders to comfort her in his absence.

Moving

Moss, Marissa. 2006. *Amelia's Notebook*. New York: Simon and Schuster.

> When Amelia moves away and misses her friends, she begins to write in her diary about her new life in a new school.

Viorst, Judith. 1995. *Alexander, Who's Not (Do You Hear Me? I Mean It!) Going to Move*. New York: Simon and Schuster.

> Alexander returns in this book detailing his discontent with moving a thousand miles away. Despite his efforts at devising plan after plan so he can stay, the move takes place. This story follows his journey and feelings throughout the process of moving.

Wagner, Anke. 2012. *Tim's Big Move*. New York: NorthSouth.

> Tim is nervous about moving, but his friend Pico is even more afraid. Pico gets jealous when Tim makes new friends. This book explores the worries and fears that children have when moving to a new town and a new school.

New Baby

Broach, Elise. 2005. *What the No-Good Baby Is Good for*. New York: Putnam.

When John's mom decides to call his bluff and pretends to make his baby sister "go somewhere else," John reconsiders just how bad the baby is. John's mom allows him to vent and helps him work through his negative feelings about having a new sibling.

Danzig, Dianne. 2009. *Babies Don't Eat Pizza: The Big Kids' Book about Baby Brothers and Baby Sisters*. New York: Dutton.

Focusing on siblings and new babies, this book covers the period of waiting for baby and follows through taking the newborn home. The author explores multiple topics including becoming a brother or sister, prematurity, adoption, special-needs babies, feeding, and general newborn care.

Falwell, Cathryn. 1999. *We Have a Baby*. New York: Clarion.

This book follows one family's journey of having a new baby, taking children through the process of having a baby, coming home, and what is required in the daily care of a baby.

Katz, Karen. 2006. *Best Ever Big Sister*. New York: Grossett and Dunlap.

An older sibling realizes how many things a new baby cannot do. By the end of the story, the big sister realizes that the baby will soon be able to do more things.

Starting School

Cohen, Miriam. 1989. *Will I Have a Friend?* New York: Aladdin.

A father's reassurance is not enough to help Jim feel more comfortable on his first day of kindergarten. It is not until he finds another child to befriend that he starts believing that he is able to make friends and enjoy his first day.

Couric, Katie. 2000. *The Brand New Kid*. New York: Doubleday.

This is a story of a child who is teased when he comes to a new school. *The Brand New Kid* teaches the importance of accepting others.

George, Lucy. 2011. *Back to School Tortoise*. Chicago, IL: Albert Whitman.

Tortoise is nervous about going back to school but soon finds that he can be brave even though he is worried about making friends and failing. Going back to school is not as bad as he has imagined.

Henkes, Kevin. 2000. *Wemberly Worried*. New York: Greenwillow.

Wemberly worries about everything, from spilling her juice to snakes in the heater vent. She is especially nervous about her first day of school and finds comfort in another classmate who also worries incessantly.

Hennesey, B. G. 2006. *Mr. Ouchy's First Day*. New York: Putnam.

A twist on an old theme, this book explains the first-day-of-school jitters from a teacher's perspective. The teacher and his students find common ground through humor, laughing at Mr. Ouchy's silly name.

McGhee, Alison. 2002. *Countdown to Kindergarten.* Orlando, FL: Harcourt.
After hearing all the "rules" from an experienced first grader, the main character is especially worried because she cannot tie her shoes. Readers also learn to count as the little girl goes through many antics to master tying her shoes.

Northway, Jennifer. 2006. *See You Later, Mum!* London: Frances Lincoln.
This story follows one a little boy as he learns to be more confident about going to school and leaving his mother. He soon discovers other little boys who feel the same as he does, and they reassure each other until Friday when the boys are able to leave their mothers more easily.

Wing, Natasha. 2001. *The Night before Kindergarten.* New York: Scholastic.
Much preparation goes into the start of school: buying supplies, packing lunches, posing for pictures; but, the hardest part of all is saying goodbye. This book helps prepare kindergarteners for the first day of school and offers a glimpse into how parents feel as they wave goodbye.

Winget, Susan. 2005. *Tucker's Four-Carrot School Day.* New York: HarperCollins.
A father talks to his young son about being scared to go to school, but offers encouragement that he can do it. The son soon finds himself painting, playing, napping, and enjoying a snack, forgetting all about his first-day jitters.

Secrets: Distinguishing between Good and Bad

Moore-Mallinos, Jennifer. 2011. *Let's Talk: Have You Got a Secret?* Brighton, East Sussex, UK: Book House.
For older children, this book discusses the difference between a good secret and a bad secret. The author helps children identify the difference between those secrets that need to be told and those that are harmless.

Separation and Change

Binch, Caroline. 2005. *The Princess and the Castle.* London: Red Fox.
Genevieve is a little girl whose father was lost at sea. Ever since then she has been unable to overcome her own fear of the ocean. The illustrations and text provide children with a thoughtful story about loss and healing.

Daly, Jude. 2006. *To Everything There Is a Season.* Grand Rapids, MI: Eerdmans.
This book uses a familiar Bible verse to explore the natural seasons of life and death. Every life has a beginning and end; this book helps the reader experience life's pleasures and sorrows.

Deacon, Alexis. 2003. *Beegu.* New York: Farrar, Straus, and Giroux.

In *Beegu,* readers connect with a small alien who is lost, lonely, and feeling unloved. He searches for someone to help, only to be turned away time and again. Eventually he finds a playground of school children who cheer him up and reduce his feelings of rejection.

Hughes, Shirley. 2010. *Don't Want to Go!* Somerville, MA: Candlewick.

A little girl finds it hard to separate from her parents and struggles even more about returning home after having a good time at the babysitter's. This book offers practical ideas to help children deal with separation anxiety.

Jarrett, Clare. 2008. *Arabella Miller's Tiny Caterpillar.* Cambridge, MA: Candlewick.

This book explores the feelings children may have about the absence of someone or something they love. A small caterpillar leaves but returns as a beautiful butterfly.

Juster, Norton. 2005. *The Hello, Goodbye Window.* New York: Hyperion.

A child's imagination and the "magic" of a special window help her to cope with the daily transitions of people who are present in everyday life. Looking at change through her special window helps her understand her feelings.

Karst, Patrice. 2000. *The Invisible String.* Marina del Rey, CA: DeVorss.

Written for preschool children, this book offers a unique perspective of the concept of connectedness and love. Children can begin to understand that, even when someone is not present, connection and love are still there.

McCormick, Wendy. 2002. *Daddy, Will You Miss Me?* New York: Simon and Schuster.

A small boy is sad when he learns his dad will be going away on a business trip for four weeks. His mom finds tangible things for her son to do to help pass the time. This book offers reassurance to anxious young children who may be experiencing separation from their parents.

Sendak, Maurice. 1988. *Where the Wild Things Are.* New York: HarperCollins.

This classic invites readers into the never-ending imagination of a young boy who gets sent to his room for being mischievous. It offers a message that helps children "run away" from their misbehavior and focus their energy in a productive imaginative way.

Taback, Simms. 2003. *Joseph Had a Little Overcoat.* New York: Penguin.

This book looks Joseph's experience of being frugal and the ability for someone to make something out of nothing. It helps young readers think of different perspectives that one can have about material possessions.

Zolotow, Charlotte. 1997. *When the Wind Stops.* New York: HarperCollins.

A boy asks why the day must end, and his mother explains that in the natural world things do not end but continue with change. *When the Wind Stops* offers children a first look at natural science and the environmental changes on Earth.

Violence

Holmes, Margaret, and Sasha Mudlaff. 2001. *A Terrible Thing Happened.* Washington, DC: Magination Press.

Sherman the raccoon witnesses a traumatic event but is supported through his interaction with a caring adult. Sherman learns to deal with his sadness and anger over what he experienced, and his process of understanding can help children come to terms with their negative feelings and emotions.

Books and Articles for Adults

Arnold, Cheryl, and Ralph Fisch. 2011. *The Impact of Complex Trauma on Development.* New York: Jason Aronson.

Arnold and Fisch describe what happens cognitively, emotionally, behaviorally, and relationally to people who are repeatedly traumatized in childhood.

Bailey, Michelle. 2011. *Parenting Your Stressed Child.* Oakland, CA: New Harbinger Publications.

This book for parents and caregivers includes ideas for helping children learn skills for regulating body-sensory responses.

Beaty, Janice. 2006. *50 Early Childhood Guidance Strategies.* Upper Saddle River, NJ: Pearson.

This book includes ideas for developing competence-focused guidance plans.

Bilmes, Jenna. 2011. *Beyond Behavior Management: The Six Life Skills Children Need.* 2nd ed. St Paul, MN: Redleaf.

Bilmes presents a strengths-based approach to guiding and managing young children's behavior by helping them build and use essential life skills.

Blaustein, Margaret, and Kristine Kinniburgh. 2010. *Treating Traumatic Stress in Children and Adolescents.* New York: Guilford Press.

Grounded in theory and research on complex childhood trauma, this book provides an accessible, flexible, and comprehensive framework for intervention with children and adolescents and their caregivers.

Brennar, Avis. 1997. *Helping Children Cope with Stress.* San Francisco, CA: Jossey-Bass.

This book reasserts the value of childhood and provides the information needed to help children deal with life's problems.

Davis, Martha, Elizabeth Eshelman, and Matthew McKay. 2007. *The Relaxation and Stress Reduction Handbook for Kids,* 6th ed. Oakland, CA: New Harbinger Publications.

This volume contains ideas for helping children learn skills for regulating body-sensory responses.

Epstein, Ann. 2011. *Me, You, and Us: Social-Emotional Learning in Preschool.* Washington, DC: NAEYC (copublished with HighScope).

Me, You, and Us explores areas of social-emotional learning and offers numerous teaching strategies and suggestions for professional development. It also includes ideas for developing competence-focused guidance plans and for helping children learn skills for regulating body-sensory responses.

Fitzgerald Rice, Kathleen, and Betsy Groves. 2005. *Hope and Healing: A Caregiver's Guide to Helping Young Children Affected by Trauma.* Washington, DC: Zero to Three.

A guide for early childhood professionals who care for children in a variety of early care and education settings. The authors define trauma and help readers recognize its effects on young children, and they offer resources for working with traumatized children and their families.

Fox, Jennifer. 2008. *Your Child's Strengths.* New York: Penguin.

Written for parents, this book provides ideas for understanding and supporting children's assets from a strengths-based perspective.

Foxman, Paul. 2004. *The Worried Child: Recognizing Anxiety in Children and Helping Them Heal.* Alameda, CA: Hunter House.

Foxman's book includes ideas for helping children learn skills for regulating body-sensory responses.

Gartrell, Daniel. 2012. *Education for a Civil Society: How Guidance Teaches Young Children Democratic Life Skills.* Washington, DC: NAEYC.

Gartrell offers ideas for developing competence-focused guidance plans.

Gil, Eliana, ed. 2010. *Working with Children to Heal Interpersonal Trauma: The Power of Play.* New York: Guilford Press.

This book describes what post-traumatic play looks like and how it can foster resilience and coping. The authors share effective strategies for engaging hard-to-reach children and building trusting therapeutic relationships.

Greenland, Susan. 2010. *The Mindful Child.* New York: Free Press.

The author offers ideas to extend the benefits of mindfulness training in children, with age-appropriate exercises, songs, games, and fables.

Honig, Alice. 2009. *Little Kids, Big Worries: Stress Busting Tips for Early Childhood Classrooms.* New York: Paul H. Brookes.

Little Kids, Big Worries gives professionals the tools they need to help children develop the early social and academic skills needed for school success.

Hyson, Marilou. 2004. *The Emotional Development of Young Children: Building an Emotion-Centered Curriculum.* 2nd ed. New York: Teachers College Press. This book for teachers focuses on using research-based practices to create and sustain a curriculum mode that supports various aspects of emotional development in young children. Activities are linked to program outcomes including the Head Start Outcomes Framework.

Jacobson, Tamar. 2008. *Don't Get So Upset!* St. Paul, MN: Redleaf. Jacobson examines the uncomfortable emotions providers feel when children exhibit strong feelings, especially anger, fear, and grief. The book challenges teachers to reflect on their own emotional histories and to find strategies for responding to children in ways that support children's emotional health and development.

Jaycox, Lisa, Lindsey Morse, Terri Tanielian, and Bradley Stein. 2006. *How Schools Can Help Students Recover from Traumatic Experiences: A Tool Kit for Supporting Long-Term Recovery.* Westport, CT: Rand. This tool kit provides information and a compendium of programs available to schools that help support the long-term recovery of traumatized children.

Karr-Morse, Robin. 2012. *Scared Sick: The Role of Childhood Trauma in Adult Disease.* New York: Basic Books. *Scared Sick* explores the multiple influences of childhood trauma on adult disease.

Katz, Janice E. 2013. *Guiding Children's Social and Emotional Development: A Reflective Approach.* Upper Saddle River, NJ: Pearson. Readers will find ideas for developing competence-focused guidance plans in this book.

Katz, Lilian, and Diane McClellan. 1991. *The Teacher's Role in the Social Development of Young Children.* Urbana, IL: ERIC Clearinghouse on Elementary and Early Childhood Education. Available at http://www.eric.ed.gov/PDFS/ED331642.pdf. This guide describes the many ways that teachers can contribute to young children's social development. It emphasizes the importance of speaking to children warmly and directly, using matter-of-fact, straightforward language.

Levin, Diane. 1994. *Teaching Young Children in Violent Times: Building a Peaceable Classroom.* Cambridge, MA: Educators for Social Responsibility. Levin offers ideas for helping children learn skills for regulating body-sensory responses.

Loy, Marty. 2010. *Children and Stress: A Handbook.* Duluth, MN: Whole Person Associates.

This book provides an overview of childhood stress and a wide array of creative activities that can be used to help children gain control over their stress, healthy coping strategies, learn new stress management skills, and value the benefits of relaxation.

Mooney, Carol. 2005. *Use Your Words: How Teacher Talk Helps Children Learn.* St. Paul, MN: Redleaf.

The author examines the ways early childhood teachers talk to children, pointing out commonly missed opportunities to support cognitive development, develop receptive and expressive language, and aid children in their primary developmental task of making sense of the world.

Oehlberg, Barbara. 1996. *Making It Better.* St. Paul, MN: Redleaf.

Making It Better offers information on how difficult life circumstances can affect children physically and emotionally. The author suggests multiple activities to help children with self-healing, empathy, and empowerment.

Perry, Bruce, and Maia Szalavitz. 2006. *The Boy Who Was Raised a Dog: What Traumatized Children Can Teach Us about Loss, Love, and Healing.* New York: Basic Books.

The authors tell the stories of traumatized children and their transformations.

Shapiro, Lawrence E., and Robin K. Sprague. 2009. *The Relaxation and Stress Reduction Workbook for Kids: Help for Children to Cope with Stress, Anxiety, and Transitions.* Oakland, CA: Instant Help Books.

This workbook helps children learn skills for regulating body-sensory responses.

Steele, William, and Cathy Malchiodi. 2012. *Trauma-Informed Practices with Children and Adolescents.* New York: Routledge.

Steele and Malchiodi synthesize research and provide guidelines for best practices in trauma-informed care. Their work contains case studies, research reviews, activities and methods for intervention, and resources for processionals.

Wickelgren, Ingrid. 2012. "Changing a Child's Mind." *Scientific American.* 23(4): 46–58.

This article includes ideas for helping children learn skills for regulating body-sensory responses.

Websites

Adverse Childhood Experiences (ACE) Study Site and Organization
www.acestudy.org/index.html
The site reviews the ACE study, which looked at the effects of adverse childhood experiences from childhood to adulthood.

American Academy of Experts in Traumatic Stress (AAETS)
www.aaets.org
This organization and its website provide information on the impact of traumatic stress on children and adults. AAETS offers membership options for professionals, training, and expert resource lists.

American Academy of Pediatrics (AAP)
www.aap.org
AAP provides research findings and policy reviews to support new strategies addressing the detrimental effects of toxic stress.

Area Health Education Center (AHEC), Washington State University Extension
http://extension.wsu.edu/ahec/pages/default.aspx
The AHEC provides support and research-based information for health-related initiatives. A major focus of the center is the implementation of trauma-informed care practices and research focusing on extending adverse childhood experiences screening in public school systems.

Center for Prevention and Early Intervention Policy (CPEIP), Florida State University
www.cpeip.fsu.edu
CPEIP focuses on maternal and child health and early childhood issues. The center provides numerous resources for professionals working with young children.

Center for the Study of Traumatic Stress
www.cstsonline.org
From research to intervention, the center focuses on the impact of war, including deployments, injury, and loss, and its effects on parenting and family function.

Center on the Developing Child, Harvard University
http://developingchild.harvard.edu
The center serves as a research unit and clearinghouse for developmental science. The site contains several multimedia features detailing how children develop and how adversity affects their development. The site also offers downloadable working papers related to child development, accessible at http://developingchild.harvard.edu/resources/reports_and_working_papers.

These papers include the following topics.

- "Children's Emotional Development Is Built into the Architecture of Their Brains" (2004)

  This report presents an overview of the scientific research on how a child's capacity to regulate emotions develops in a complex interaction with his environment and ongoing cognitive, motor, and social development. It then discusses the implications of this research for policies affecting young children, their caregivers, and service providers.

- "Young Children Develop in an Environment of Relationships" (2004)

  This report summarizes the most current and reliable scientific research on the impact of relationships on all aspects of a child's development, and identifies ways to strengthen policies that affect those relationships in the early childhood years.

- "Excessive Stress Disrupts the Architecture of the Developing Brain" (2005)

  This report explains how significant adversity early in life can alter—in a lasting way—a child's capacity to learn and to adapt to stressful situations, how sensitive and responsive caregiving can buffer the effects of such stress, and how policies could be shaped to minimize the disruptive effects of toxic stress on young children.

- "Early Exposure to Toxic Substances Damages Brain Architecture" (2006)

  This report summarizes research on which toxins present the greatest risk at various stages of brain development, addresses popular misconceptions about the relative risk and safety of some common substances, and suggests policies that can help reduce exposure to toxins during development.

- "The Timing and Quality of Early Experiences Combine to Shape Brain Architecture" (2007)

  This report summarizes in clear language the most recent scientific advances in understanding the importance of sensitive periods on brain development, and the implications of those findings for policy.

- "Establishing a Level Foundation for Life: Mental Health Begins in Early Childhood" (2008, 2012)

  Sound mental health provides an essential foundation of stability that supports all other aspects of human development—from the formation of friendships and the ability to cope with adversity to the achievement of success in school, work, and community life. This report explains in clear language why understanding how emotional well-being can be strengthened or disrupted in early childhood can help policy makers promote the kinds of environments and experiences that prevent problems and remediate early difficulties so they do not destabilize the developmental process.

- "Maternal Depression Can Undermine the Development of Young Children" (2009)
  Serious depression in parents and caregivers can influence the well-being of children in their care and seriously weaken the development of children's brains. This report examines the effects of maternal depression on young children and offers recommendations for interventions.

- "Persistent Fear and Anxiety Can Affect Young Children's Learning and Development" (2010)
  Ensuring that young children have safe, secure environments in which to grow, learn, and develop healthy brains and bodies is not only good for the children themselves but also builds a strong foundation for a thriving, prosperous society. This report examines why these experiences have the potential to affect how children learn, solve problems, and relate to others.

- "Building the Brain's 'Air-Traffic Control' System: How Early Experiences Shape the Development of Executive Function" (2011)
  Children are born with the potential to develop skills that help them control impulses, stay focused, and make plans, but these skills must be learned. This report examines executive function skills and the role that early experiences play in developing these skills.

Center on School, Family, and Community Partnerships, Johns Hopkins University
www.csos.jhu.edu/p2000/center.htm
This center conducts and disseminates research, programs, and policy analyses to help parents, educators, and members of communities work together to improve schools, strengthen families, and enhance student learning and development.

Center on the Social and Emotional Foundations for Early Learning (CSEFEL), Vanderbilt University
www.csefel.vanderbilt.edu
CSEFEL is focused on promoting the social-emotional development and school readiness of young children birth to age five. Funded by the Office of Head Start and Child Care Bureau, CSEFEL disseminates research and evidence-based practices to early childhood programs across the country.

Centers for Disease Control (CDC)

www.cdc.gov/NCCDPHP/ACE/publications.htm

The CDC offer helpful downloads and publications related to the topic of adverse childhood experiences.

Child Trauma Academy (CTA)

www.childtrauma.org

The CTA translates emerging findings about the human brain and child development into practical implications for the ways we nurture, protect, enrich, educate, and heal children.

Child Traumatic Stress Network

http://www.nctsnet.org/nctsn_assets/pdfs/what_is_child_traumatic_stress.pdf

This article discusses child traumatic stress and its effects.

Devereux Center for Resilient Children

www.devereux.org

Devereux provides information on strengths-based social and emotional well-being. The organization focuses on supporting strategies to build resiliency. Assessments for resiliency capacity are found in the widely used DECA assessment for young children.

Healthy Children

www.healthychildren.org

Healthy Children offers excellent information on emotional wellness, family life, nutrition, sleep, and more. Resources are intended for professionals and parents.

Mind in the Making

http://mindinthemaking.org

Mind in the Making shares the science of early learning with those who care about children's learning and development, with a focus on the brain and its link to emotional development in children.

National Association for the Education of Young Children (NAEYC)

www.naeyc.org

The NAEYC provides resources and tools for parents, caregivers, and teachers of young children birth through age eight.

National Association of School Psychologists (NASP) School Safety and Crisis Resources

www.nasponline.org/resources/crisis_safety

The website provides materials for educators and parents to use while helping children cope with anxiety related to local and global crisis and methods to promote peace with children.

National Center for Trauma-Informed Care

http://www.samhsa.gov/nctic/

The center provides research support and policy directives advancing models and methods of implementation for trauma-informed care.

National Child Care Information Center (NCCIC)

www.csrees.usda.gov/nea/family/part/childcare_part_nccic.html

NCCIC is a clearinghouse and technical assistance center that links families, providers, policy makers, researchers, and the public to early care and education information.

National Child Traumatic Stress Network (NCTSN)

www.nctsnet.org

NCTSN provides information and resources for improving the care of children traumatized by war or other disasters. The organization's website includes tips for educators and parents, press releases, publications, and many other materials related to traumatic events and children. The NCTSN provides options for leadership and collaborative initiatives for clinicians and professionals in all areas of traumatic stress. Policy papers and clinical vignettes to explain complex trauma and to demonstrate its effects upon children and families can also be found on the website.

Search Institute

www.search-institute.org

Search Institute provides extensive documentation on resilience and developmental assets for multiple age groups, families, and communities.

Spaces for Children

www.spacesforchildren.com

This website provides photographs of well-designed child care programs, before and after pictures, and articles. Spaces for Children focuses on developmentally appropriate environments: rich places of learning that are child directed and teacher efficient.

North Carolina Child Care Health and Safety Resource Center

www.healthychildcarenc.org

The center compiles a wide variety of links to resources on a variety of topics related to children and their health.

The Strengthening Families Initiative

www.cssp.org/reform/strengthening-families

This initiative of the Center for the Study of Social Policy works to build protective factors into early childhood systems and programs to prevent child abuse and neglect. The website provides substantial information on protective factors and offers resources for strengthening community-based partnerships.

Technical Assistance Center on Social Emotional Intervention for Young
    Children (TACSEI)
    http://www.challengingbehavior.org
    TACSEI offers resources and research to improve the social-emotional
    outcomes for young children.
Wilder Research
    www.wilder.org
    Wilder Research gathers and interprets facts and trends in order to help
    families and communities thrive, get at the core of community concerns, and
    uncover issues that are overlooked or poorly understood.
Zero to Three
    www.zerotothree.org
    Zero to Three provides numerous resources that support the healthy
    development and well-being of infants, toddlers, and their families. Its Policy
    Network is a vehicle for professionals to use their knowledge and expertise
    to influence public policy.

References

Akrofi, Amma, Jeanne Swafford, Carole Janisch, Xiaoming Liu, and Vance Durrington. 2008. "Supporting Immigrant Students' Understanding of U. S. Culture through Children's Literature." *Childhood Education* 84(4): 209–218.

Anda, Robert, and Vincent Felitti. 2012. Adverse Childhood Experiences (ACE) Study. ww.acestudy.org/index.html.

Arnold, Cheryl, and Ralph Fisch. 2011. *The Impact of Complex Trauma on Development*. New York: Jason Aronson.

Bailey, Michelle. *Parenting Your Stressed Child*. 2011. Oakland, CA: New Harbinger Publications.

Beaty, Janice. 2006. *50 Early Childhood Guidance Strategies*. Upper Saddle River, NJ: Pearson.

Berson, Ilene, and Jennifer Baggerly. 2009. "Building Resilience to Trauma" *Childhood Education* 85(6): 375–379.

Biglan, Anthony, Brian Flay, Dennis Embry, and Irwin Sandler. 2012. "The Critical Role of Nurturing Environments for Promoting Human Well-Being." *American Psychologist* 67(4): 257–271.

Bilmes, Jenna. 2011. *Beyond Behavior Management: The Six Life Skills Children Need*. 2nd ed. St Paul, MN: Redleaf.

Birckmayer, Jennifer, Anne Kennedy, and Anne Stonehouse. 2008. *From Lullabies to Literature: Stories in the Lives of Infants and Toddlers*. Washington, DC: NAEYC.

Blair, Clancy, and C. Cybele Raver. 2012. "Child Development in the Context of Adversity." *American Psychologist* 67(4): 309–318.

Blaustein, Margaret, and Kristine Kinniburgh. 2010. *Treating Traumatic Stress in Children and Adolescents*. New York: Guilford Press.

Brazelton, T. Berry, and Stanley I. Greenspan. 2000. *The Irreducible Needs of Children: What Every Child Must Have to Grow, Learn, and Flourish*. Cambridge, MA: Perseus.

Bredekamp, Sue. 2010. *Effective Practices in Early Childhood Education: Building a Foundation*. Upper Saddle River, NJ: Pearson.

Bredekamp, Sue, and Carol Copple, eds. 2009. *Developmentally Appropriate Practice in Early Childhood Programs*. 3rd ed. Washington, DC: NAEYC.

Breslin, Deidre. 2005. "Children's Capacity to Develop Resiliency: How to Nurture It." *Young Children* 60(1): 47–48, 50–52.

Briere, John. 2005. *Trauma Symptom Checklist for Young Children (TSCYC): Professional Manual*. Odessa, FL: Psychological Assessment Resources, Inc.

Brooks, Robert, and Sam Goldstein. 2001. *Raising Resilient Children: Fostering Strength, Hope, and Optimism in Your Child.* Lincolnwood, IL: Contemporary Books.

Bruce, Nefertiti, and Karen B. Cairone. 2011. *Socially Strong, Emotionally Secure.* Silver Spring, MD: Gryphon House.

Bruno, Holly E. 2011. "The Neurobiology of Emotional Intelligence: Using Our Brain to Stay Cool under Pressure." *Young Children* 66(4): 22–27.

Burman, Lisa. 2009. *Are You Listening? Fostering Conversations that Help Young Children Learn.* St. Paul, MN: Redleaf.

Carlson, Frances. 2006. *Essential Touch: Meeting the Needs of Young Children.* Washington, DC: NAEYC.

Carlson, Frances, and Bryan Nelson. 2006. "Reducing Aggression with Touch." *Dimensions of Early Childhood* 34(3): 9–15.

Center on the Developing Child. 2004a. "Young Children Develop in an Environment of Relationships." Working paper no. 1. Cambridge, MA: Harvard.

Center on the Developing Child. 2004b. "Children's Emotional Development Is Built into the Architecture of Their Brains." Working paper no. 2. Cambridge, MA: Harvard.

Center on the Developing Child. 2005. "Excessive Stress Disrupts the Architecture of the Developing Brain." Working paper no. 3. Cambridge, MA: Harvard.

Center on the Developing Child. 2006. "Early Exposure to Toxic Substances Damages Brain Architecture." Working paper no. 4. Cambridge, MA: Harvard.

Center on the Developing Child. 2007. "The Timing and Quality of Early Experiences Combine to Shape Brain Architecture." Working paper no. 5. Cambridge, MA: Harvard.

Center on the Developing Child. 2008. "Establishing a Level Foundation for Life: Mental Health Begins in Early Childhood." Working paper no. 6. Cambridge, MA: Harvard.

Center on the Developing Child. 2009. "Maternal Depression Can Undermine the Development of Young Children." Working paper no. 8. Cambridge, MA: Harvard.

Center on the Developing Child. 2010. "Persistent Fear and Anxiety Can Affect Young Children's Learning and Development." Working paper no. 9. Cambridge, MA: Harvard.

Center on the Developing Child. 2011. "Building the Brain's 'Air-Traffic Control' System: How Early Experiences Shape the Development of Executive Function." Working paper no. 11. Cambridge, MA: Harvard.

Center on the Developing Child. 2012a. "Establishing a Level Foundation for Life: Mental Health Begins in Early Childhood." Working paper no. 6, rev. ed. Cambridge, MA: Harvard.

Center on the Developing Child. 2012b. "The Science of Neglect: The Persistent Absence of Responsive Care Disrupts the Developing Brain." Working paper no. 12. Cambridge, MA: Harvard.

Chu, Ann T., and Alicia F. Lieberman. 2010. "Clinical Implications for Traumatic Stress from Birth to Age Five." *Annual Review of Clinical Psychology* 6: 469–694.

Cole, Susan. 2007. *Helping Traumatized Children Learn: Supportive School Environments for Children Traumatized by Family Violence,* rev. ed. Boston: MA: Advocates for Children.

Crawford, Patricia, and Sherron K. Roberts. 2009. "Ain't Gonna Study War No More." *Childhood Education* 85(6): 360–374.

Curtis, Deb, and Margie Carter. 2003. *Designs for Living and Learning: Transforming Early Childhood Environments.* St. Paul, MN: Redleaf.

Davis, Martha, Elizabeth Eshelman, and Matthew McKay. 2007. *The Relaxation and Stress Reduction Handbook for Kids.* 6th ed. Oakland, CA: New Harbinger Publications.

DeViney, Jessica, Sandra Duncan, Sara Harris, Mary Ann Rody, and Lois Rosenberry. 2010. *Inspiring Spaces for Young Children.* Silver Spring, MD: Gryphon House.

Dunn, Rita, Kenneth Dunn, and Janet Perrin. 1993. *Teaching Young Children through Their Individual Learning Styles.* Upper Saddle River, NJ: Pearson.

Epstein, Ann. 2011. *Me, You, and Us: Social-Emotional Learning in Preschool.* Washington, DC: NAEYC (copublished with HighScope).

Eliason, Claudia, and Loa Jenkins. 1994. *A Practical Guide to Early Childhood Curriculum.* 5th ed. New York: Macmillan.

Florez, Ida R. 2011. "Developing Young Children's Self-Regulation through Everyday Experiences." *Young Children* 66(4): 46–54.

Fox, Jennifer. 2008. *Your Child's Strengths.* New York: Penguin.

Foxman, Paul. 2004. *The Worried Child: Recognizing Anxiety in Children and Helping Them Heal.* Alameda, CA: Hunter House.

Galinsky, Ellen. 2010. *Mind in the Making: The Seven Essential Life Skills Every Child Needs.* New York: HarperCollins.

Gardner, Howard E. 2006. *Multiple Intelligences: New Horizons in Theory and Practice.* New York: Basic Books.

Gartrell, Daniel. 2012. *Education for a Civil Society: How Guidance Teaches Young Children Democratic Life Skills.* Washington, DC: NAEYC.

Gillanders, Cristina, and Dina Castro. 2011. "Storybook Reading for Young Dual Language Learners." *Young Children* 66(1): 91–94.

Gillespie, Linda G., and Sandra Petersen. 2012. "Rituals and Routines." *Young Children* 67(4): 76–77.

Gillespie, Linda G., and Nancy L. Seibel. 2006. "Self-Regulation: A Cornerstone of Early Childhood Development." *Young Children* 61(4): 34–39.

Ginsburg, Kenneth. R. 2006. *A Parent's Guide to Building Resilience in Children and Teens: Giving Your Child Roots and Wings.* Elk Grove Village, IL: The American Academy of Pediatrics.

Gonzalez-Mena, Janet. 2008. *Diversity in Early Care and Education: Honoring Differences.* New York: McGraw-Hill.

Grasso, Damion, Julian Ford, and Margaret Briggs-Gowan. 2012. "Early Life Trauma Exposure and Stress Sensitivity in Young Children." *Journal of Pediatric Psychology* 38(1): 94–103.

Greenland, Susan. 2010. *The Mindful Child.* New York: Free Press.

Greenman, Jim. 2005. *What Happened to MY World? Helping Children Cope with Natural Disaster and Catastrophe.* Watertown, MA: Bright Horizons.

Greenman, Jim. 2005. *Caring Spaces, Learning Places.* Redmond, WA: Exchange Press.

Gunnar, Megan, Adriana Herrera, and Camelia E. Hostinar. 2009. "Stress and Early Brain Development." *Encyclopedia on Early Childhood Development* 1–8. Montreal, Quebec: Centre of Excellence for Early Childhood Development.

Hendrick, Joanne. 1967. "The Pleasure of Meaningful Work." *Young Children* 22(6): 373–380.

Hendrick, Joanne. 2003. *Total Learning: Developmental Curriculum for the Young Child.* 6th ed. Upper Saddle River, NJ: Pearson.

Hodas, Gordon. 2006. *Responding to Childhood Trauma: The Promise and Practice of Trauma-Informed Care.* Pennsylvania Office of Mental Health and Substance Abuse Services. http://www.dpw.state.pa.us/ucmprd/groups/public/documents/manual/s_001585.pdf

Holmes, Thomas H., and Richard H. Rahe. 1967. "The Social Readjustment Rating Scale." *Journal of Psychosomatic Research* 11(12):213–218.

Honig, Alice. 2009. *Little Kids, Big Worries: Stress Busting Tips for Early Childhood Classrooms.* New York: Paul H. Brookes.

Hyson, Marilou. 2004. *The Emotional Development of Young Children: Building an Emotion-Centered Curriculum.* 2nd ed. New York: Teachers College Press.

Jablon, Judy R., and Michael Wilkinson. 2006. "Using Engagement Strategies to Facilitate Children's Learning and Success." *Young Children* 61(2): 12–16.

Jacobson, Tamar. 2008. "Don't Get So Upset!" *Help Young Children Manage Their Feelings by Understanding Your Own.* St. Paul, MN: Redleaf.

Jalongo, Mary R. 2004. *Young Children and Picture Books.* 2nd ed. Washington, DC: NAEYC.

Jalongo, Mary R. 2008. *Learning to Listen, Listening to Learn.* Washington, DC: NAEYC.

Jewett, Jan, and Karen Peterson. 2002. "Stress and Children." *ERIC Digest.* Champaign, IL: ERIC Clearinghouse on Elementary and Early Childhood Education. www.ericdigests.org/2003–4/stress.html.

Kacev, Glenda, and Sylvia Roth. 2012. *Bal Yoga for Kids.* San Diego: Bal Yoga.

Karr-Morse, Robin. 2012. *Scared Sick: The Role of Childhood Trauma in Adult Disease.* New York: Basic Books.

Katz, Janice E. 2013. *Guiding Children's Social and Emotional Development: A Reflective Approach.* Upper Saddle River, NJ: Pearson.

Katz, Lilian. 1992. "Early Childhood Programs: Multiple Perspectives on Quality." *Childhood Education* 69(2): 66–71.

Katz, Lilian. 1993. "Dispositions as Educational Goals." *ERIC Digest.* Champaign, IL: ERIC Clearinghouse on Elementary and Early Childhood Education. www.ericdigests.org/1993/dispositions/html

Katz, Lilian, and Sylvia Chard. 1989. *Engaging Children's Minds: The Project Approach.* Norwood, NJ: Ablex Publishing.

Katz, Lilian, and Diane McClellan. 1991. *The Teacher's Role in the Social Development of Young Children.* Urbana, IL: ERIC Clearinghouse on Elementary and Early Childhood Education. Available at www.eric.ed.gov/PDFS/ED331642.pdf.

Kersey, Katharine C., and Marie L. Masterson. 2013. *101 Principles for Positive Guidance with Young Children.* Upper Saddle River, NJ: Pearson.

Kinniburgh, Kristine, Margaret Blaustein, Joseph Spinazzola, and Bessel van der Kolk. 2005. "Attachment, Self-Regulation, and Competency: A Comprehensive Intervention Framework for Children with Complex Trauma." *Psychiatric Annals* 35(5): 424–430.

Kostelnik, Marjorie, Anne Soderman, and Alice P. Whiren. 2011. *Developmentally Appropriate Curriculum: Best Practices in Early Childhood Education.* 5th ed. Upper Saddle River, NJ: Pearson.

Kutash, Krista, Albert J. Duchnowski, and Nancy Lynn. 2006. *School-Based Mental Health: An Empirical Guide for Decision-Makers.* Gainesville, FL: University of Florida Press.

Landy, Sarah. 2002. *Pathways to Competence: Ensuring Healthy Social and Emotional Development in Young Children.* Baltimore, MD: Paul H. Brookes.

Lerner, Richard M., Francine Jacobs, and Donald Wertlieb. 2004. *Applied Developmental Science*. Thousand Oaks, CA: Sage Publications.

Levin, Diane. 1994. *Teaching Young Children in Violent Times: Building a Peaceable Classroom*. Cambridge, MA: Educators for Social Responsibility

Loy, Marty. 2010. *Children and Stress: A Handbook for Parents, Teachers, and Therapists*. Duluth, MN: Whole Person Associates.

Marion, Marian. 2011. *Guidance of Young Children*. 8th ed. Upper Saddle River, NJ: Pearson.

McMullen, Mary B., Susan Dixon, and Eva M. Shivers. 2006. "Building on Common Ground: Unifying Practice with Infant/Toddler Specialists through a Mindful, Relationship-Based Approach." *Young Children* 61(4): 46–52.

Miller, Regina, and Joan Pedro. 2006. "Creating Respectful Classroom Environments." *Early Childhood Education Journal* 33(5):293–299.

Mooney, Carol G. 2005. *Use Your Words: How Teacher Talk Helps Children Learn*. St. Paul, MN: Redleaf.

Olds, Anita R. 2001. *Child Care Design Guide*. New York: McGraw-Hill.

O'Neill, Linda, Francis Guenette, and Andrew Kitchenham. 2010. "'Am I Safe Here and Do You Like Me?' Understanding Complex Trauma and Attachment Disruption in the Classroom." *British Journal of Special Education* 37(4): 190–197.

Osofsky, Joy. 2004. *Young Children and Trauma: Interventions and Treatment*. New York: Guilford.

Perry, Bruce. 1997. "Incubated in Terror: Neurodevelopmental Factors in the 'Cycle of Violence.'" In *Children, Youth and Violence: The Search for Solutions*, 124–149. New York: Guilford.

Perry, Bruce. 2007. *Early Childhood and Brain Development: How Experience Shapes Child, Community, and Culture*. DVD. Houston, TX: Child Trauma Academy.

Pizzolongo, Peter J., and Amy Hunter. 2011. "I Am Safe and Secure: Promoting Resilience in Young Children." *Young Children* 66(2): 67–69.

Readdick, Christine, and Kathy Douglas. 2000. "More than Line Leader and Door Holder." *Young Children* 55(6): 63–70.

Rice, Phillip. 1992. *Stress and Health*. Pacific Grove, CA: Brooks/Cole Publishing.

Riley, David, Robert San Juan, Joan Klinkner, and Ann Ramminger. 2008. *Social and Emotional Development: Connecting Science and Practice in Early Childhood Settings*. St. Paul, MN: Redleaf, copublished with NAEYC.

Roberts, Sherron K., and Patricia Crawford. 2008. "Literature to Help Children Cope with Family Stressors." *Young Children* 63(5): 12–17.

Roberts, Sherron K., and Patricia Crawford. 2009. "Children's Literature Resources on War, Terrorism, and Natural Disasters for Pre-K to Grade 3." *Childhood Education* 85(6): 385–391.

Selye, Hans. 1956. *The Stress of Life*. New York: McGraw-Hill.

Shapiro, Lawrence E., and Robin K. Sprague. 2009. *The Relaxation and Stress Reduction Workbook for Kids: Help for Children to Cope with Stress, Anxiety, and Transitions*. Oakland, CA: Instant Help Books.

Shonkoff, Jack P. 2010. "Building a New Biodevelopmental Framework to Guide the Future of Early Childhood Policy." *Child Development* 81(1):357–376.

Shonkoff, Jack P., and Deborah Phillips, eds. 2000. *From Neurons to Neighborhoods: The Science of Child Development*. Washington, DC: National Academy Press.

Stanford, Beverly, and Kaoru Yamamoto, eds. 2001. *Children and Stress*. Olney, MD: Association for Childhood Education International (ACEI).

Steele, William, and Cathy Malchiodi. 2012. *Trauma-Informed Practices with Children and Adolescents*. New York: Routledge.

Stone, Jeannette G. 2001. *Building Classroom Community: The Early Childhood Teacher's Role*. Washington, DC: NAEYC.

Summers, Susan Janko, and Rachel Chazan-Cohen. 2012. *Understanding Early Childhood Mental Health*. Baltimore, MD: Paul H. Brookes.

Sutherland, Zena. 1997. *Children and Books*. 9th ed. New York: Longman.

Thelen, Peggy, and Tammy Klifman. 2011. "Using Daily Transition Strategies to Support All Children." *Young Children* 66(4): 92–98.

Volk, Dinah, and Sisi Long. 2005. "Challenging Myths of Deficit Perspective: Honoring Children's Literacy Resources." *Young Children* 60(6): 12–19.

Webster, Paula S., and Yvette R. Harris. 2009. "Working with Children Who Have Experienced War, Terrorism, and Disaster." *Childhood Education* 85(6): 364–369.

Werner, Emmy. 1984. "Resilient Children." *Young Children* 40(1): 68–72.

Werner, Emmy. 1990. "Protective Factors and Individual Resilience." In *Handbook of Early Childhood Intervention*, 97–116. New York: Cambridge University Press.

Wheeler, Edyth. 2004. *Conflict Resolution in Early Childhood: Helping Children Understand, Manage, and Resolve Conflict*. Upper Saddle River, NJ: Pearson.

Wickelgren, Ingrid. 2012. "Changing a Child's Mind." *Scientific American* 23(4): 46–58.

Wolf, Kathy Goetz. 2012. *Living the Protective Factors: How Parents Keep Their Children Safe and Families Strong*. Chicago, IL: Strengthening Families Illinois and Be Strong Families.

Yamamoto, Kaoru, and Deborah Byrnes. 1987. "Primary Children's Ratings of the Stressfulness of Experiences." *Journal of Research in Childhood Education* 2(2): 117–121.

Zeece, Pauline D. 1998. "Books for Children: Disasters!" *Early Childhood Education Journal* 25(3): 189–192.

Zeece, Pauline D. 2000. "Meeting Children's Needs with Quality Literature: Part One." *Early Childhood Education Journal* 28(3): 175–180.

Zeece, Pauline D. 2001. "Meeting Children's Needs with Quality Literature: Part Two." *Early Childhood Education Journal* 28(4): 237–241.

Zeece, Pauline D., and Jeanne Stolzer. 2002. "Books for Children: Creating Literature Safety Zones for Young Children." *Early Childhood Education Journal* 30(1): 47–52.

Zero to Three. 2012. *Diagnostic Classification of Mental Health and Developmental Disorders of Infancy and Early Childhood,* revised. Washington, DC: Zero to Three. www.zerotothree.org

Index

School readjustment, 149–150, 166–167

Science, 138

Secrets, 167

Seibel, Nancy L., 93

Self-awareness, 31, 41

Self-care skills, 45, 113, 135

Self-competence, 56, 70, 48, 58, 137
    building, 111–136
    defined, 112
    experiences, 114–115
    ideas for practice, 134–136
    portfolio of, 115–134
    stress, trauma, and, 112–113

Self-confidence, 7, 106

Self-defense, 45

Self-efficacy, 31, 41, 97, 112

Self-esteem, 127

Self-evaluation, 127

Self-regulation skills, 9, 48, 89–111, 137
    activities in the classroom, 107–108
    children's responses, 90–91
    ideas for practice, 108–110
    managing stress symptoms, 92–96
    modifying responses, 96–107
    understanding, 93–96

Self-reliance, 7, 55

Self-sufficiency, 21, 56, 113, 129

Selye, Hans, 13

Sensitivity, 94–95

Sensory cues, 103

Sensory integration, 25

Sensory sensitivity, 98, 103–105, 111, 137

Sensory stimulation, 19–21, 23, 25, 31–32,
    36, 42, 94, 97, 108

Sensory triggers, 38

Separation, 22, 27, 51, 139, 141, 145, 149,
    167–169

Sexual abuse, 17

Sharing, 76, 91

Siblings, 149–150, 157, 166

Silliness, 36

Singing, 106

Skills, 140

Sleep problems, 44, 90

Smoking, 40

Social cues, 137

Social cultures, 114

Social learners, 63

Social manipulation, 91

Social Readjustment Scale, 26

Social responsibility, 7

Social skills, 14, 31, 37, 45, 47–49, 53, 55–56,
    66, 76, 81–86, 108, 111, 113–114, 118,
    122–123, 139, 142–143

Spatial learners, 63–64

Stanford, Beverly, 23, 44

Steele, William, 43, 47–48, 55, 91–92, 123

Stolzer, Jeanne, 143

Stomachaches, 45

Stone, Jeannette, 72, 81

Story starters, 110

Strengths-based profiles, 65–69

Stress triggers, 91, 93, 104

Stress, 7–8, 143
    acute, 14, 16–17, 26, 90
    children's experience of, 32–39
    children's responses, 40–45
    chronic, 14, 16–17, 26, 37, 39, 45, 47, 58,
        75, 90
    complex trauma, 27
    defining, 13–14
    developmental, 14–17
    ideas for practice, 28–30, 49–51
    impact on children, 28
    learning from, 45–47
    long-term exposure to, 39–40
    measuring, 25–26
    mechanics of, 31–51
    multisensory experience, 16, 23–24
    negative, 17–20
    physical responses, 25–26, 32–33
    positive, 17–20
    self-competence and, 112–113
    sources for children, 20–23, 149–150
    toxic, 19, 26, 28, 37, 39–49
    understanding, 11–30
    vulnerability to, 24–25
    working with children, 47–49

Stroke, 40

Stuffed animals, 103

Stuttering, 44

Substance abuse, 22, 40

Summers, Susan Janko, 16, 19, 23, 45, 82,
    90, 117, 123